MMC: Developing Communicative Competence in ESL

Part 1. Lessons One through Eleven

Mary Newton Bruder
and Gary Esarey

University of Pittsburgh Press for the English Language Institute
of the University of Pittsburgh

Pitt Series in English as a Second Language—13

Distributed by the University of Pittsburgh Press, 127 N. Bellefield Ave., Pittsburgh, Pa. 15260

Library of Congress Cataloging in Publication Data

Bruder, Mary Newton, 1939–
MMC: Developing communicative competence in ESL.

(Pitt series in English as a second language)
Includes bibliographical references and index.
1. English language—Text-books for foreign speakers.
I. Esarey, Gary R. II. Title. III. Title: M.M.C.
IV. Series.
PE1128.B736 1985 428.2'4 84-21975
ISBN 0-8229-8213-7 (Part 1)
ISBN 0-8229-8214-5 (Part 2)

Contents

Lesson Seven ***The Football Game***

Lesson Eight ***The Telephone***

Lesson Nine ***At the Bank***

Lesson Ten ***The Used Car***

Lesson Eleven ***Credit Cards***

Preface to the Revised Edition

After twenty years' involvement with language teaching and having seen many language teaching fads come and go, we still firmly believe that most students with zero proficiency in a language learn best by learning the grammar first, and that each structure learned should be used communicatively from the beginning. The theoretical framework, Paulston's "The Sequencing of Structural Pattern Drills," remains the same.[1]

To summarize the Paulston classification, a set of materials purporting to teach the structural patterns of a language ought to contain three classes of drills: mechanical drills to train the student's tongue and ear to the forms of the language, meaningful drills which allow the students some freedom to choose answers of their own in using the prescribed structures, and lastly communicative drills which allow the student maximum freedom to communicate and add new information to the common body of knowledge of the speech community. (The speech community is here defined as the members of a class in English as a second or foreign language.) The major difference between the types of drills is the decreasing control by the teacher of the response by the student. Meaningful and communicative drills are by definition individual response types and require more class time than mechanical ones.

The major objective of the text is to provide maximum opportunity for communication *by the students*, which means that the majority of class time should be spent in "student talk." The teacher must react to and encourage reaction to what the students say, and the teacher's role in directing the class activities should diminish as the students' proficiency increases.

Paulston's warning that communicative drills are still *drills* needs to be emphasized. Just because the students can answer questions fluently and grammatically in the classroom is no guarantee that they will be able to do so in "the real world." To help the students bridge the gap, we have included a series of communicative activities modeled on the discussion by Wilga Rivers in "Talking off the Tops of Their Heads."[2] The exercises consist of solving problems in situations in which the students are likely to find themselves; for example, getting a telephone, opening a bank account.

The major changes from the first edition represent comments from both teachers and students over ten years of classroom use. Some of the patterns have been reordered, taking better account of difficulty. The generalization comes before any drilling. We found that drilling first hindered the slower students who couldn't figure out what was going on. This way everyone starts out equally. We have tried very hard to contextualize the drills around the central topic or at least a central vocabulary theme. This was not always possible, but there should be fewer "stream of consciousness" exercises. We have put the long dialogue at the end of each chapter as an introduction to

1. Christina Bratt Paulston, "The Sequencing of Structural Pattern Drills," *TESOL Quarterly* 5 (Sept. 1971):197–208.
2. Wilga M. Rivers, "Talking Off the Tops of Their Heads," *TESOL Quarterly* 6 (March 1972):71–81.

the communicative activities. This should help the teachers who didn't know what to do with it. We chopped the book into two parts, which should help those who complained it was too heavy. We have kept many of the topics because they have been useful to the students and have updated the others. We hope your students will approve.

Acknowledgments

We are grateful to all the people who helped with this revision; we would not have been able to complete the task without their assistance. Special thanks go to Holly Deemer Rogerson and Linda Schmandt who spent long hours looking for glitches. We also thank the people who helped at the "MMC checking" marathon: Deborah Fink, Patricia Furey, Robert Henderson, Paul Lux, Lionel Menasche, Joe Polifroni, and Bob Weide. Judy Vernick and her staff at the Language Lab did a wonderful job on the tapes. Karen Billingsley and JoEllen Walker typed and retyped uncomplainingly. Finally, we want to thank our families who put up with our absences on evenings and weekends for so long. Aidah, Arini, Harris, Mary Beth, and Charlie—this is for you.

Suggestions for Using the Text

The text consists of twenty-two lessons of English grammar designed for students who know no English through the intermediate level—0 to 65 on the Michigan Test of English Proficiency. Lessons One through Eleven are in Part 1, Lessons Twelve through Twenty-Two are in Part 2. We firmly believe that students who know no English should start with the grammar and should use each grammar pattern communicatively from the start. Hence MMC—Mechanical, Meaningful, Communicative.

Each lesson begins with a few lines of introduction which describe the context or theme of the lesson. The introductory passage is followed by a vocabulary list. The major part of the lesson is the presentation and drilling of the patterns. Each new pattern is introduced by a brief exchange of dialogue to place the teaching point in context. a simple generalization explains the structure to be practiced in the exercises which follow. Every lesson ends with a long dialogue and a communicative exercise that helps link structure to communicative settings and cultural information.

I. Introductions

The introductory passages are meant to be read aloud by the teacher.

A. Read the Introduction aloud as the students read along silently.

B. Ask for and answer student questions about vocabulary items.

II. Vocabulary

The lists are for the students' use at home. The students should look up the words in advance so that little class time need be spent on vocabulary, and also so that the students can do the grammar exercises with vocabulary that they know. (We do not believe that students should practice patterns of which they do not know the meaning.)

III. Mini Dialogues

A. Read the exchange aloud as the students read along silently. We do not have the students read the dialogues aloud because it is wasteful of class time, and it provides an imperfect model for the other students. The students profit more by practicing the dialogues individually in the laboratory.

B. Point out (or elicit) examples of the pattern to be studied in the upcoming generalization and exercises.

IV. Generalizations

The grammatical generalizations are placed before the mechanical exercises. In this way all students may obtain a firm grasp of the teaching point before they move on to the exercises.

Lengthy explanations concerning the rules are wasteful of class time and are often unnecessary. Putting the model sentences on the board and allowing the students to "figure out" the rules gives the students additional opportunity to talk, and they often give simple, comprehensible explanations which are more helpful to the less proficient students than wordy discussions by the teacher. If you would like more information about a particular point, we recommend Quirk & Greenbaum, *A Concise Grammar of Contemporary English* (New York: Harcourt Brace Jovanovich, 1973) as a teacher reference.

There is a minimum amount of linguistic information for the simple reason that it doesn't seem to be necessary for the students' performance. As often as possible, the structures and transformations are presented visually for the students' use at home. Sometimes the generalizations ask questions which the student should be able to answer (see p. 23). The correct answers are given in parentheses following the question.

Not all of the occurrences of each pattern are presented in the text. For example, the students are told that *already* is used with affirmative sentences; *yet* with negative and interrogative sentences. Obviously, this does not account for such items as: Has he already come?, but at this level of proficiency, such subtleties might cause confusion and are best left to intermediate and advanced texts.

V. Mechanical Drills (M1)

The term *mechanical* refers to the automaticity of the oral response by the student. We do not believe (and Paulston does not intend) that the drills be devoid of meaning in a lexical sense. Even in a mechanical drill, the students must know what they are saying; that is the reason for assigning the vocabulary for study prior to any of the drills.

These drills are usually repetition or simple substitution exercises, practiced for the purpose of learning the form of the new pattern. They should always be done chorally and at a very rapid pace—no more than a minute and a half per drill. As soon as the students can do the M1 drills with ease, erase the model from the board and proceed to the next set of drills.

With classes of very low proficiency we have found a tendency to resist the M1 drills around Lesson Ten or so. The resistance is not an indication that the students can do the drills, but they seem to want to get on to more interesting exercises. At this point, we emphasize use of the M1 drills in the lab and spend more class time on the M2 and C. The M1 drills should still precede the others, however, either in class or in the lab.

VI. Mechanical-testing Drills (M1T)

The purpose of these drills is to contrast the new pattern with ones learned previously and to ensure that the students can manipulate the distinctions. These drills also should be done chorally (except for ones which have two possible arrangements of the answers) and very rapidly in order to keep the pace brisk and to arrive as quickly as possible at the last sets of drills which are much more interesting for the students. The answers are given for the M1 and M1T drills so that the students can practice them at home.

VII. Meaningful (M2) and Communicative (C) Drills

These drills are completely individual, and the students are allowed to answer with any grammatically correct response which is appropriate to the speech situation. We usually insist that the students provide long, full-sentence answers in the M2 drills, and short, conversationally appropriate answers in the C drills, but since the objective is communicative competence the C drills should be an approximation of "real language." "Real language" in many contexts consists of short answers to direct questions. If the students are to acquire "real conversational English" they must be encouraged to respond from their earliest lessons in short answers. The students also need to know the appropriateness of certain responses—either rude or polite, etc., and only you can provide that information.

A word of caution concerning the C drills: sometimes the students will say anything that comes to them with no regard for the real situation. It is imperative that answers to the C drills be "true" in order for them to be effective. It is occasionally necessary to ask the student "Really?" and ask him to give another answer if his first one was contrived.

Your reaction to the students' responses can often clarify the grammatical point. In a present perfect continuous drill, a student was asked what he'd been doing all morning, with the teacher expecting a reply such as "I've been studying English all morning." Instead he responded "I've been sleeping all morning"—a clear indication that he hadn't grasped the function of the tense. The teacher replied "Oh really, are you sleeping now?" and saw the "lightbulbs" come on over several members of the class who must have been having the same problem. There were no more mistakes of that kind for the remainder of the class. It is absolutely essential that you respond to mistakes of this kind in a natural conversational manner. Only as a last resort should you retreat to linguistic information in correcting responses to M2 and C drills, because mistakes (other than in form) at this point indicate that the students have not understood the usage. The best way to correct usage mistakes is to make them see what kind of misunderstanding can occur.

VIII. Drills, Modeling the Drills, and Drilling

It is wasteful of class time to tell the students that they are to "change the sentence to the negative." What you want them to do is get into the drill with the least amount of effort and the maximum of correct responses. By using gestures you can indicate what you say and then what they are to respond. After two, or at the most, three examples, the students will respond if your modeling is clear. This technique also reinforces the students' analogyzing ability and helps you spot those who may be having trouble with the pattern. We always go back to the beginning examples when starting the drill with the entire class, however, because then everyone has a chance to begin with familiar material and the slower students do better.

The mechanical drills should take no more than two minutes each, and some much less time than that. A fast pace will decrease the boredom and get you to the M2 and C drills more quickly.

Most of the M1 and M1T drills should be done chorally to keep the pace fast. There is sufficient time for individual practice with the M2 and C drills. Some of the M1 and M1T drills are constructed to be done individually and are so marked in the text.

The M1 drills are by definition a presentation of new material. However, once a pattern has been presented, subsequent lessons frequently use these patterns in contrast in the M1 drills. Testing (M1T) drills focus on the pattern currently under study. For example, "singular/plural" distinctions are taught in Lesson One. After that, singular/plural *object* cues are not considered as a test, but merely a review of the earlier pattern.

Parentheses should be filled by names of the students or their countries or items pertaining to the particular class. Sometimes the class should be divided into groups for responses and this is indicated by G1 and G2. For the sake of conserving space, the abbreviations *Rep* (Repeat) and *Sub* (Substitute) have been used.

Some of the C drills have several items and then conclude with *etc*. These drills should be completed by mixing up the models given and adding similar items to fit your class.

IX. Summary Dialogue

The summary dialogues are intended as contextualized reviews of the patterns presented in the lesson and, after the first few lessons, an introduction to the communicative activities. The students can use information and phrases from the dialogues in the discussions and role plays which make up the bulk of the communicative activities.

They should be read aloud (in class or in lab) as the students follow along. They are not intended for memorization, although the students may want to memorize certain useful phrases.

X. Communicative Activities

The communicative activities are an attempt to take the students beyond the use of language in drills to using language to communicate needs and wishes. The situations reflect those encountered by our students and should be adapted to individual class situations. In conducting these activities, teacher and students should be primarily aware of communicative errors—inappropriate gestures, rude-sounding intonation. Grammatical errors should be corrected only if they interfere with communication or if they sound particularly awful to the teacher.

Many of the dialogues and communicative activities can serve as introductions to discussions (sometimes rather chaotic) of cross-cultural differences. The major difficulty here for the teacher is directing the discussions so that the students do not lose sight of the fact that difference does not mean necessarily "good" or "bad." The teacher must also keep in mind the fact that students who use these opportunities to unduly criticize the United States may be having "culture shock" problems.

XI. Styles of Language

Following Lessons Seven and Fourteen there are short dialogues in contrasting styles. The informal style dialogues should be practiced as listening comprehension exercises, but not practiced orally, because until the students become quite proficient, they will mix the styles, causing great confusion and further complicating their attempts to communicate.

The teacher should help the students analyze the variables involved in each situation (age, sex, familiarity) and translate some of the striking differences between the styles. It is not intended that a great deal of time be spent on the dialogues; one class hour on each set of variations serves to give students the comprehension skill necessary to their feeling at ease outside of the classroom situation.

XII. Homework

We have found that written work is a positive reinforcement of the spoken patterns and that it should follow closely class presentation and practice of each pattern. Instead of endless construction of dittoed exercises, many of the instructors have found that assigning the M2 and C drills as homework is very useful. There is, in addition, the *Student's Workbook of Grammar Exercises* by D. G. Akhand which can be obtained from the University of Pittsburgh Press.

XIII. Tailoring the Textbook for Individual Classes

Most of the patterns in Lessons One through Four are meant for students who have never studied English. With classes of higher proficiency, they should be done very briefly as review, if at all. The teacher of advanced beginning classes should pick items such as the *wh* questions or indefinite pronouns, with which even quite proficient students will have trouble, and skip the rest or have the students practice in the laboratory.

MMC: Developing Communicative Competence in ESL

Lesson One

First Day of Class

Introduction

Carlos and Chen are students at a large American university. It is in a large city. They are foreign students; Carlos is from Latin America and Chen is from Asia. The campus is confusing and the boys are lost. All the buildings are gray.

Comprehension Questions

1. Is the university big?
2. Where is the university?
3. Who are Chen and Carlos?
4. Where is Chen from? Carlos?
5. Why are they lost?

Vocabulary Look up these words before you do the lesson.

Nouns

answer
boy
building
campus
capital
class
classroom
country (nation)
girl
house
man
professor
room
student
teacher
weather
woman

Adverb

here

Adjectives

beautiful
big
cheap
clean
cold
confused
confusing
difficult
dirty
easy
expensive
fat
foreign
friendly
handsome
hot
intelligent
large
long
lost
nice
open
polite
pretty
short
small
tall
thin
ugly
white

SECTION ONE

BE—Present Tense

Part A-1. Third Singular + BE + Adjective

Generalization

The sentences in the following exercises represent a basic English sentence pattern:

	Subject	+	Verb	+	Complement

Most of the sentences in this book will have the same basic structure.

Lesson 1A	Noun	+	BE	+	Adjective
Example:	The campus		is		confusing.

---

1. Rep: The campus is confusing.
M1 The university is big.
The building is gray.
The boy is handsome.
The boy is lost.
The professor is fat.
The girl is beautiful.
The student is confused.

2. Rep: The campus is big.
M1 Sub: small — S: The campus is small.
beautiful — The campus is beautiful.
confusing — The campus is confusing.
large — The campus is large.
dirty — The campus is dirty.
big — The campus is big.

3. Rep: The boy is tall.
M1 Sub: girl — S: The girl is tall.
student — The student is tall.
woman — The woman is tall.
instructor — The instructor is tall.
professor — The professor is tall.
man — The man is tall.

Rep: Repeat Sub: Substitute S: Student

4. (Picture Cue)

M1 T: confusing — S: The campus is confusing.
handsome — The boy is handsome.
beautiful — The girl is beautiful.
white — The house is white.
small — The car is small.
long — The pencil is long.

5. (Picture Cue)

M2 T: Describe the campus. — S: The campus is (confusing) (large).
Describe the car. — The car is (expensive) (cheap).
Describe the house. — The house is (beautiful).
Describe the pencil.
Describe the room.
Describe the building.
Describe the university.

T: Describe the professor. — S: The professor is (tall) (confused).
Describe the student. — The student is (fat).
Describe the woman.
Describe the boy.
Describe the girl.
Describe the instructor.

Part A-2. Pronouns

Examples:

The university is big.	It is confusing.
Carlos is a new student.	He is from Latin America.
The tall woman is an instructor.	She is a graduate student.

Generalization

Use the pronoun *he* to refer to masculine subjects, *she* for feminine subjects, and *it* for nonhuman subjects.

Note the difference between the written and spoken forms.

Listen to your teacher say these sentences:

Written	*Spoken*
He is from Latin America.	He's from Latin America.
It is cheap.	It's cheap.
She is beautiful.	She's beautiful.

T: Teacher

6.	Rep:	The campus is big.	It's big.
M1		The campus is confusing.	It's confusing.
		The campus is clean.	It's clean.
		The campus is pretty.	It's pretty.
		The campus is new.	It's new.
		The campus is nice.	It's nice.

7.	Rep:	The boy is from Asia.	He's from Asia.
M1		The boy is from China.	He's from China.
		The boy is tall.	He's tall.
		The boy is handsome.	He's handsome.
		The boy is confused.	He's confused.
		The boy is lost.	He's lost.

8.	Rep:	The girl is from Latin America.	She's from Latin America.
M1		The girl is from Colombia.	She's from Colombia.
		The girl is tall.	She's tall.
		The girl is polite.	She's polite.
		The girl is intelligent.	She's intelligent.
		The girl is beautiful.	She's beautiful.

9.	T:	The campus is nice.	S: It's nice.
M1T		The girl is nice.	She's nice.
		The building is nice.	It's nice.
		The boy is nice.	He's nice.
		The university is nice.	It's nice.
		The woman is nice.	She's nice.
		The country is nice.	It's nice.

10.		(Picture Cue)	
M2	T:	Describe the building.	S: It's (new) (big).
		Describe the girl.	She's (pretty) (lost).
		Describe the boy.	He's (tall).
		Describe the building.	
		Describe the university.	
		Describe the pencil.	
		Describe the campus.	
		Describe the boy.	
		Describe the professor.	
		Describe the girl.	
		Describe the student.	
		Describe the woman.	
		Describe the instructor.	

11.	T:	Describe your country.	S: It's (beautiful) (clean).
C		Describe the capital of your country.	
		Describe your university.	
		Describe your room.	

Describe your apartment.
Describe your friend.
Describe your brother.
Describe your sister.
Describe your instructor.

Part A-3. Question and Affirmative Short Answer

Examples:

Is the campus confusing?	Yes, it is.
Is the woman beautiful?	Yes, she is.
Is the boy handsome?	Yes, he is.

Generalization

Statement: The campus [is] confusing.

Question: [Is] the campus confusing? Answer: Yes, it is.

Note: The voice goes up at the end of these questions.

---

12. **M1** Rep:

Is the campus confusing?.	Is it confusing?
Is the building tall?	Is it tall?
Is the woman beautiful?	Is she beautiful?
Is the boy handsome?	Is he handsome?

13. **M1T**

T:	S:
The building is confusing.	Is the building confusing?
It is clean.	Is it clean?
It's pretty.	Is it pretty?
The girl is confused.	Is the girl confused?
She's lost.	Is she lost?
The professor is polite.	Is the professor polite?
He's friendly.	Is he friendly?

14. **M1** Rep:

Is the room small?	Yes, it is.
Is the building tall?	Yes, it is.
Is the campus confusing?	Yes, it is.
Is the girl beautiful?	Yes, she is.
Is the instructor intelligent?	Yes, she is.
Is the woman thin?	Yes, she is.
Is the boy handsome?	Yes, he is.
Is the boy from Asia?	Yes, he is.

15. (Picture Cue—Affirmative)

M1T T: clean — G1: Is (the campus) clean? — G2: Yes, it is.
beautiful — Is (the girl) beautiful? — Yes, she is.
handsome — Is (the boy) handsome? — Yes, he is.
fat
tall
thin
small
confusing
short
dirty
long
handsome
pretty

Note to teacher: Collect pictures using the nouns and adjectives presented previously so the students can construct questions which are answered *yes*. Exercises marked G1, G2 should be done with the class divided in groups.

16. (Picture Cue—Affirmative)

M2 T: Ask a question about the girl. — S1: Is the girl (fat) (lost)? — S2: Yes, she is.
T: Ask a question about the room. — S1: Is the room (small)? — S2: Yes, it is.

T: Ask a question about the boy.
Ask a question about the professor.
Ask a question about the woman.
Ask a question about the student.
Ask a question about the instructor.
Ask a question about the house.
Ask a question about the building.
Ask a question about the campus.
Ask a question about the girl.

Part A-4. Negative and Short Answer

Chen: Is the class here?
Carlos: No, it isn't. The classroom isn't open.

Generalization

The class is not here.
The class isn't here.

Not follows BE. The contraction is common in speech.

Short answer: No, it isn't.

---

17. Rep: The room isn't open.
M1
The class isn't here.
The dorm isn't clean.
The university isn't cheap.
The student isn't friendly.
The girl isn't nice.
The professor isn't here.
The man isn't fat.

18. Listen: If you hear an affirmative statement, raise one hand; if you hear a negative
M1T statement, raise two hands.

T:		S:
	The campus isn't confusing.	(2)
	The dorm is gray.	(1)
	It isn't cheap.	(2)
	He isn't a graduate student.	(2)
	The boy is intelligent.	(1)
	The girl isn't beautiful.	(2)
	The professor isn't from Asia.	(2)
	She's intelligent.	(1)

19. **M1T**

T:		S:
	The campus is confusing.	The campus isn't confusing.
	The class is difficult.	The class isn't difficult.
	The dorm is clean.	The dorm isn't clean.
	The room is open.	The room isn't open.
	The university is small.	The university isn't small.
	The boy is intelligent.	The boy isn't intelligent.
	The student is handsome.	The student isn't handsome.
	The girl is polite.	The girl isn't polite.
	The woman is beautiful.	The woman isn't beautiful.

20. **M1T**

T:		S:
	Is the professor handsome?	No, he isn't handsome.
	Is the girl tall?	No, she isn't tall.
	Is the man thin?	No, he isn't thin.
	Is the boy polite?	No, he isn't polite.
	Is the woman beautiful?	No, she isn't beautiful.
	Is the campus confusing?	No, it isn't confusing.

Exercise continues on next page.

Is the building clean?	No, it isn't clean.
Is the dorm expensive?	No, it isn't expensive.
Is the class here?	No, it isn't here.
Is the room open?	No, it isn't open.

21. (Picture Cue—Negative Answers)
M2

T:	S1:	S2:
big	Is the (campus) big?	No, it isn't big.
confusing	Is the (building) confusing?	No, it isn't confusing.
expensive		
cheap		
dirty		

T:	S1:	S2:
tall	Is the (woman) tall?	No, she isn't tall.
handsome	Is the (boy) handsome?	No, he isn't handsome.
short		
fat		
ugly		

22. Short Answers
M1

T:	S:
Is the woman beautiful?	No, she isn't.
Is the man tall?	No, he isn't.
Is the boy short?	No, he isn't.
Is the girl thin?	No, she isn't.
Is the pencil long?	No, it isn't.
Is the room clean?	No, it isn't.
Is the building clean?	No, it isn't.

23. (Picture Cue—Affirmative and Negative Answers)
M2

T:		
Ask a question about this picture.	S1: Is the building (tall) (beautiful)?	S2: No, it isn't. (Yes, it is.)
	S2: Is the woman (beautiful)?	S3: Yes, she is.

24.
C

T:	S:
Is (Pittsburgh) clean?	(Yes, it is.)
Is the university confusing?	
Is the English class difficult?	
Is the answer easy?	
Is (Pittsburgh) beautiful?	
Is the capital of your country big?	
Is the teacher tall?	(Yes, he/she is.)
Is the teacher thin?	(No, he/she isn't.)
Is ( ) handsome?	
Is ( ) intelligent?	
Is ( ) short?	
Is ( ) polite?	
Is your friend confused?	

Note to teacher: Insert names of people in the class or others known to the students.

Part B-1. Third Plural + BE + Adjective

Chen: Are the students here?
Carlos: No, They aren't. Maybe they're late.
Chen: Maybe they're lost. Maybe the professor's lost, too.
Carlos: No, the students aren't lost. And the professor . . . Wait, here they are now.

Vocabulary

Nouns	*Adjectives*	*Adverbs*
book	busy	maybe
*child	late	now
*man	young	too
*woman		
*irregular plural		

Generalization

The regular plural is formed with *-(e)s,* but there are different sounds.

Listen to the pronunciation: students
boys
campuses

Examples:

Singular: The student is lost.
Plural: The students are lost.

Note: The adjective *lost* is the same.

Note: The form of the verb BE used with the plural is *are*.

Examples:

Singular: The student is lost.
Plural: The students are lost.
Singular: The book is lost.
Plural: The books are lost.

Note: Irregular Plurals
man—men woman—women child—children

1. Listen: If you hear a singular statement, raise one hand; if you hear a plural
M1T statement, raise both hands.

T:	The university is expensive.	S:	(1)
	The books are expensive.		(2)
	The rooms are clean.		(2)
	The buildings are dirty.		(2)
	The boy is tall.		(1)
	The men are handsome.		(2)
	The women are tall.		(2)
	The boy is intelligent.		(1)
	The students are lost.		(2)

2. Rep: The boys are lost.
M1

Sub:	girls	S:	The girls are lost.
	students		The students are lost
	men		The men are lost.
	professors		The professors are lost.
	women		The women are lost.
	teachers		The teachers are lost.

Rep: The books are nice.

Sub:	dorms	S:	The dorms are nice.
	rooms		The rooms are nice.
	buildings		The buildings are nice.
	classrooms		The classrooms are nice.

3. Rep: The boys are lost.
M1

Sub:	intelligent	S:	The boys are intelligent.
	handsome		The boys are handsome.
	tall		The boys are tall.
	thin		The boys are thin.
	young		The boys are young.

4.
M1T

T:	The boy is lost.	S:	The boys are lost.
	The girl is intelligent.		The girls are intelligent.
	The boy is handsome.		The boys are handsome.
	The woman is beautiful.		The women are beautiful.
	The man is tall.		The men are tall.

T:	The building is confusing.	S:	The buildings are confusing.
	The dorm is expensive.		The dorms are expensive.
	The room is big.		The rooms are big.
	The book is difficult.		The books are difficult.
	The class is easy.		The classes are easy.

5. (Picture Cue—Plural Subjects)

M2	T: Describe the boys.	S:	The boys are (tall) (handsome).
	Describe the buildings.		The buildings are (dirty).
	Describe the girls.		
	Describe the men.		
	Describe the women.		
	Describe the books.		
	Describe the rooms.		
	Describe the buildings.		

Part B-2. Pronouns

Chen: The students are lost.
Carlos: No, they're here.

Generalization

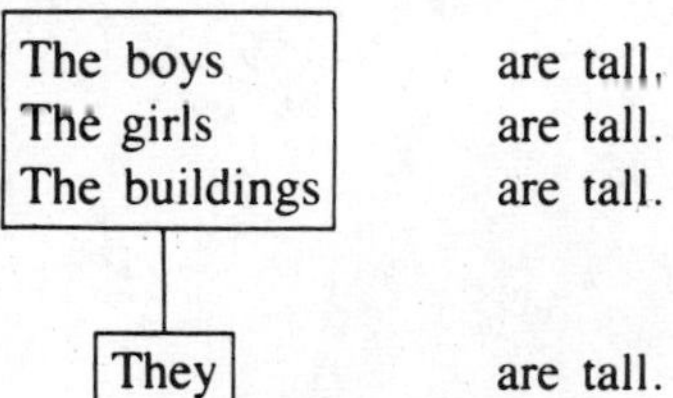
The boys are tall.
The girls are tall.
The buildings are tall.
They are tall.

They is the substitute word for all plural subjects. Note the difference between usual spoken and written forms:

Written	*Spoken*
They are tall.	They're tall.

6.	Rep: The students are lost.	They're lost.
M1	The boys are tall.	They're tall.
	The girls are ugly.	They're ugly.
	The rooms are nice.	They're nice.
	The books are expensive.	They're expensive.
	The buildings are ugly.	They're ugly.

7.	T: The buildings are tall.	S: They're tall.
M1T	The room is dirty.	It's dirty.
	The dorms are expensive.	They're expensive.
	The classroom is big.	It's big.
	The girls are pretty.	They're pretty.
	The students are intelligent.	They're intelligent.

Exercise continues on next page.

		The professors are good.	They're good.
		The boy is lost.	He's lost.

8. (Picture Cue—Singular and Plural)

M2	T:	Describe the boys.	S:	They're (confused) (lost).
		Describe the boy.		He's (handsome) (tall).
		Describe the student.		
		Describe the girls.		
		Describe the professor.		
		Describe the men.		
		Describe the woman.		
		Describe the campus.		
		Describe the building.		
		Describe the classroom.		
		Describe the dorm.		
		Describe the books.		

9.	T:	Describe the classroom.	S:	It's (big) (clean).
C		Describe the books.		They're (expensive).
		Describe the university.		
		Describe the dorms.		
		Describe the capital of your country.		
		Describe the people in (your country).		
		Describe the building.		
		Describe the students here.		
		Describe the women.		
		Describe the men.		
		Describe the teachers.		

Part B-3. Questions and Affirmative Short Answers

Example:
Are the boys lost? Yes, they are.

Generalization

Part A Statement: The boy [is] lost.

Question: [Is] the boy lost? Answer: Yes, he is.

Part B Statement: The boys [are] lost.

Question: [Are] the boys lost? Answer: Yes, they are.

---

10. Rep: Are the boys lost?
M1 Are the girls friendly?
Are the students here?
Are the teachers good?
Are the books expensive?
Are the dorms cheap?
Are the buildings confusing?

11. T: The boys are lost.
M1 The girls are nice.
The students are lost.
The teachers are friendly.
The books are cheap.
The rooms are dirty.
The dorms are expensive.
The classes are hard.

S: Are the boys lost?
Are the girls nice?
Are the students lost?
Are the teachers friendly?
Are the books cheap?
Are the rooms dirty?
Are the dorms expensive?
Are the classes hard?

12. T: The boy is lost.
M1T He's lost.
The boys are handsome.
They're handsome.
The girl is friendly.
She's friendly.
The girls are nice.
They're nice.
The room is clean.
It's clean.
The dorms are expensive.
They're expensive.

S: Is the boy lost?
Is he lost?
Are the boys handsome?
Are they handsome?
Is the girl friendly?
Is she friendly?
Are the girls nice?
Are they nice?
Is the room clean?
Is it clean?
Are the dorms expensive?
Are they expensive?

13. T: Are the books expensive?
M1 Are the rooms clean?
Are the classes hard?
Are the boys lost?
Are the students here?
Are the teachers good?

S: Yes, they are.
Yes, they are.
Yes, they are.
Yes, they are.
Yes, they are.
Yes, they are.

14. T: Is the book cheap?
M1T Are the books cheap?
Is the campus confusing?
Is the dorm clean?
Are the rooms dirty?
Are the classes hard?
Is Chen from Asia?
Are the boys lost?
Are the girls friendly?
Is the boy confused?
Is the woman from the United States?

S: Yes, it is.
Yes, they are.
Yes, it is.
Yes, it is.
Yes, they are.
Yes, they are.
Yes, he is.
Yes, they are.
Yes, they are.
Yes, he is.
Yes, she is.

Part B-4. Negative and Short Answers

Examples:
The books aren't cheap.
Are the classes easy? No, they aren't.

Notice the difference between written and spoken forms.

Written	*Spoken*
The book is not cheap.	The book isn't cheap.
The classes are not easy.	The classes aren't easy.

Contractions are not usually used in formal written style.

---

15. Rep: The books aren't cheap.
M1 The classes aren't easy.
The buildings aren't clean.
The rooms aren't open.
The students aren't here.
The boys aren't from the United States.

16. Listen: Affirmative, raise one hand; negative, raise two hands.
M1

T:		S:
	The boys are lost.	(1)
	The boys aren't lost.	(2)
	They aren't lost.	(2)
	The students aren't here.	(2)
	They're here.	(1)
	The books are cheap.	(1)
	They aren't cheap.	(2)
	The rooms are open.	(1)
	They're clean.	(1)
	The dorms aren't clean.	(2)

17. **M1**

T:		S:
	The boys are lost.	The boys aren't lost.
	The students are here.	The students aren't here.
	The teachers are friendly.	The teachers aren't friendly.
	The books are cheap.	The books aren't cheap.
	The rooms are open.	The rooms aren't open.
	The classes are hard.	The classes aren't hard.
	The dorms are expensive.	The dorms aren't expensive.

18. **M1**

Rep:		S:
	Are the students here?	No, they aren't.
	Are the boys lost?	No, they aren't.
	Are the teachers friendly?	No, they aren't.

Are the dorms nice?	No, they aren't.
Are the classes easy?	No, they aren't.
Are the books cheap?	No, they aren't.

19. (Class should be divided into groups)

	T:		G1:		G2:
M1T	T:	boys—lost	G1:	Are the boys lost?	G2: No, they aren't.
		boy—lost		Is the boy lost?	No, he isn't.
		girl—lost		Is the girl lost?	No, she isn't.
		students—here		Are the students here?	No, they aren't.
		teachers—nice		Are the teachers nice?	No, they aren't.
		girls—friendly		Are the girls friendly?	No, they aren't.
		girl—pretty		Is the girl pretty?	No, she isn't.
		room—open		Is the room open?	No, it isn't.
		books—expensive		Are the books expensive?	No, they aren't.
		campus—confusing		Is the campus confusing?	No, it isn't.
		building—open		Is the building open?	No, it isn't.
		dorms—cheap		Are the dorms cheap?	No, they aren't.
		classes—hard		Are the classes hard?	No, they aren't.

20. **C**	T:	Ask if (student) is from Hong Kong.	S1:	Is ( ) from Hong Kong?	S2: (Yes, he is) or (No, he isn't).
		Ask if ( ) is from Saudl Arabia.		Is ( ) from Saudi Arabia?	(No, she isn't. She's from Kuwait) or (Yes, she is).

T: Ask if ( ) is from Mexico.
Ask if ( ) is from China.
Ask if ( ) is from Venezuela.
Ask if the teacher is from the United States.
Ask if ( ) and ( ) are from Saudi Arabia.
Ask if ( ) is from Asia.
Ask if ( ) and ( ) are from Latin America.
Ask if ( ) is from Pittsburgh.
Ask if ( ) and ( ) are from the United States.

Part C. X + BE + Noun Phrase
Statements and Questions

Vocabulary

Nouns		*Adjectives*	
advisor	instructor	bad	engineering
assistant	laboratory (lab)	biology	good
biologist		business	graduate
chemist		chemistry	undergraduate

Example: In the classroom.

Nancy is an undergraduate. She is in the biology class. The boys are undergraduates, too. The tall woman is the biology teacher. She's a graduate student. The fat man is the lab assistant.

Part C-1. Singular Noun Phrases

Generalization

Part A & B:	The girl is	beautiful.	(Adjective)
Part C:	The girl is	a student.	(Noun)
	The girl is	an undergraduate.	(Noun)

Use *a* before a noun beginning with a consonant sound; use *an* before a noun beginning with a vowel sound.

Listen to your teacher pronounce these words: a teacher
a student
a woman
an undergraduate
an assistant

---

1. Rep: The woman is a student.

	Sub:		S:
M1	Sub:	a teacher	S: The woman is a teacher.
		an instructor	The woman is an instructor.
		a graduate student	The woman is a graduate student.
		an assistant	The woman is an assistant.
		a biology teacher	The woman is a biology teacher.
		a teaching assistant	The woman is a teaching assistant.
		an advisor	The woman is an advisor.

2. Rep: The woman is a student.

	Sub:		S:
M1T	Sub:	teacher	S: The woman is a teacher.
		assistant	The woman is an assistant.
		teaching assistant	The woman is a teaching assistant.
		instructor	The woman is an instructor.
		graduate student	The woman is a graduate student.
		advisor	The woman is an advisor.
		undergraduate advisor	The woman is an undergraduate advisor.

3. Rep: The man is a lab assistant.

M1T Sub:		S:
	tall	The man is tall.
	student	The man is a student.
	fat	The man is fat.
	graduate student	The man is a graduate student.
	instructor	The man is an instructor.
	friendly	The man is friendly.
	assistant	The man is an assistant.
	lab assistant	The man is a lab assistant
	young	The man is young.
	teacher	The man is a teacher.

4. (Picture Cue—Singular Affirmative)

M2 T: Describe the man. S: He's (tall)
Describe the woman. She's (a teacher).
Describe the girl.
Describe the boy.
Describe the building.
Describe the campus.
Describe the room.

Part C-2. Plural Noun Phrases

Example:
The boys are students.

Generalization

Singular:	The boy	is	a	student.
Plural:	The boys	are		students.

There are 4 differences in the singular and plural sentences. What are they? (boy/boys; is/are; a/∅; student/students.)

---

5. Rep: The boys are students.
M1 The girls are undergraduates.
The men are instructors.
The women are teaching assistants.
The boys are biology students.

6. Listen: If the sentence is singular, raise one hand; if the sentence is plural, raise two hands.
M1

	T		S
	The woman is a teacher.		(1)
	The women are teachers.		(2)
	The boy is an undergraduate.		(1)
	The woman is a biologist.		(1)
	The men are biologists.		(2)
	The women are instructors.		(2)
	The girl is an advisor.		(1)
	The man is a biologist.		(1)
	The men are teaching assistants.		(2)
	The boys are undergraduates.		(2)

7. M1T

T:	S:
The boy is a student.	The boys are students.
The girl is a teacher.	The girls are teachers.
The woman is an instructor.	The women are instructors.
The man is an assistant.	The men are assistants.
The professor is a biologist.	The professors are biologists.
The boy is an undergraduate.	The boys are undergraduates.
The girl is a graduate student.	The girls are graduate students.
The man is a biologist.	The men are biologists.
The woman is a professor.	The women are professors.

8. M1T

T:	S:
The boys are undergraduates.	The boy is an undergraduate.
The women are graduate students.	The woman is a graduate student.
The boys are students.	The boy is a student.
The men are biologists.	The man is a biologist.
The women are instructors.	The woman is an instructor.
The women are teachers.	The woman is a teacher.
The men are teaching assistants.	The man is a teaching assistant.
The professors are biologists.	The professor is a biologist.
The women are professors.	The woman is a professor.

9. M1T

T:	S:
The boy is a student.	The boys are students.
The girls are undergraduates.	The girl is an undergraduate.
The student is an undergraduate.	The students are undergraduates.
The professor is a biologist.	The professors are biologists.
The women are students.	The woman is a student.
The woman is a graduate student.	The women are graduate students.
The man is an instructor.	The men are instructors.
The boys are students.	The boy is a student.
The woman is a teaching assistant.	The women are teaching assistants.

10. M2

T: boy—student

S1: Is the boy a student?
S2: (Yes, he is.)
(No, he isn't. He's a teacher.)

T: men—graduate students

S1: Are the men graduate students?
S2: (Yes, they are.)
(No. They aren't. They're undergraduates).

girls—students
woman—biologist
men—instructors
man—graduate student
woman—teaching assistant
man—lab assistant
women—graduate students
boys—biology students

11. T: Ask if ( ) is a biologist.
M2

S1: (Is ( ) a biologist?
S2: (Yes, he is.)
(No, he isn't. He's a student.)

T: Ask if ( ) and ( ) are graduate students.

S1: Are ( ) and ( ) graduate students?
S2: (No. They aren't. They are undergraduates.)

Ask if ( ) is an undergraduate.
Ask if ( ) is a teaching assistant.
Ask if ( ) and ( ) are professors.
Ask if ( ) is a lab assistant.
Ask if ( ) and ( ) are graduate students.
Ask if ( ) is an instructor.
Ask if ( ) and ( ) are undergraduates.
Ask if ( ) and ( ) are teaching assistants.
Ask if ( ) is a professor.

Part C-3. Adjective and Noun

Examples:
The young woman is a good student.
The young women are good students.

12. Rep: The young woman is a student.
M1 Sub: fat — S: The fat woman is a student.
tall — The tall woman is a student.
beautiful — The beautiful woman is a student.
friendly — The friendly woman is a student.
thin — The thin woman is a student.
short — The short woman is a student.
young — The young woman is a student.

13. Rep: The young woman is a good student.
M1 Sub: bad — S: The young woman is a bad student.
new — The young woman is a new student.
graduate — The young woman is a graduate student.

Exercise continues on next page.

biology	The young woman is a biology student.
chemistry	The young woman is a chemistry student.

Note: *a* student/*an* engineering student

an instructor/*a* good instructor

a or *an* agrees with the following word.

---

14. Rep: The tall boy is a business student.
M1T Sub:

Sub	S
biology	The tall boy is a biology student.
girl	The tall girl is a biology student.
thin	The thin girl is a biology student.
engineering	The thin girl is an engineering student.
woman	The thin woman is an engineering student.
fat	The fat woman is an engineering student.
chemistry	The fat woman is a chemistry student.
man	The fat man is an chemistry student.
tall	The tall man is a chemistry student.

Note: The adjective does not change when the noun is plural.

---

15. Listen: The girl is a graduate student.
M1 Repeat: The girls are graduate students.
Listen: The woman is a good teacher.
Repeat: The women are good teachers.
Listen: The man is a lab assistant.
Repeat: The men are lab assistants.
Listen: The boy is a bad student.
Repeat: The boys are bad students.

16. **M1**

T	S
The young man is a good teacher.	The young men are good teachers.
The fat man is a graduate student.	The fat men are graduate students.
The tall woman is a bad instructor.	The tall women are bad instructors.
The young woman is a teaching assistant.	The young women are teaching assistants.
The tall boy is a good student.	The tall boys are good students.
The fat man is a lab assistant.	The fat men are lab assistants.
The thin girl is a bad student.	The thin girls are bad students.

17. (Use Picture Cues—Affirmative)

M2 T: man—professor
women—students
girl—assistant
boys—students
men—instructors
woman—biologist
girl—student
man—teacher
women—advisors

S: The (young) man is a (good) professor.
The (short) women are (graduate) students.

18. T: Describe the capital of your country.
C Describe the people in the capital.
Describe the buildings in the capital.
Describe your university in your country.
Describe the campus of your university.
Describe the university buildings.
Describe your professors.
Describe the students.
Describe your English classes here.
Describe Pittsburgh.
Describe the buildings here.
Describe your (room) here.
Describe your friends here.

S: It's (a beautiful) (a big) city.
They're (friendly) (nice) people.

Part D. Second Person

Carlos: Excuse me, I think I'm lost. Is this Allen Hall?
Nancy: Yeah. Are you in Biology 110?
Chen: Yes.
Nancy: Then you're not lost. This is it.

Generalization

You is singular and plural.

Examples:

Are you in the class? Yes, I am.
(No, I'm not.)
Are you in the class? Yes, we are.
(No, we aren't.)

When speaking, say *you're*; when writing, use *you are*.

---

1. Rep: You're from Latin America.
M1 You're from Asia.
You're undergraduates.
You're handsome.
You're tall.
You're in biology.
You're in the classroom.

Note: You are lost. How is the question formed?

2.	T:	You're lost.	S:	Are you lost?
M1		You're from Asia.		Are you from Asia?
		You're from the U.S.		Are you from the U.S.?
		You're confused.		Are you confused?
		You're undergraduates.		Are you undergraduates?
		You're teachers.		Are you teachers?
		You're a graduate student.		Are you a graduate student?

3.	T:	You're lost.	S:	Are you lost?
M1T		She's lost.		Is she lost?
		It's lost.		Is it lost?
		He's a good student.		Is he a good student?
		They're good instructors.		Are they good instructors?
		You're confused.		Are you confused?
		He's from Asia.		Is he from Asia?

Note: You are lost. How is the negative formed?

4.	Rep:	You aren't lost.		
M1	Sub:	confuseu	S:	You aren't confused.
		a teacher		You aren't a teacher.
		a student		You aren't a student.
		from Latin America		You aren't from Latin America.
		biologists		You aren't biologists.
		graduate students		You aren't graduate students.

5.	T:	You're from Asia.	S:	You aren't from Asia.
M1T		He's a good student.		He isn't a good student.
		They are friendly.		They aren't friendly.
		She's confused.		She isn't confused.
		It's cheap.		It isn't cheap.
		You're lost.		You aren't lost.
		We're from Latin America.		We aren't from Latin America.

Part E. First Person

Nancy: Are you from around here?
Carlos: No, I'm from Latin America.
Chen: And I'm from Asia.

Generalization

When speaking, say *I'm;* when writing, use *I am*.

---

1. Rep: I'm from Asia.
M1 Sub: a student — S: I'm a student.
confused — I'm confused.
lost — I'm lost.
an undergraduate — I'm an undergraduate.
from Latin America — I'm from Latin America.
a new student — I'm a new student.

2. T: Are you an undergraduate or a graduate student? — S: I'm (a graduate student).
M2
Are you from Asia or from Latin America? — I'm from (Latin America).
Are you a biologist or a chemist? — I'm a ( ).
Are you a biology student or a chemistry student?
Are you from ( ) or ( )?
Are you an instructor or an advisor?
Are you a math student or an English student?
Are you an undergraduate or a graduate student?

Generalization

I + other people = *We*

Example:
You and I are students. We're students.

Note: When you mention someone else and yourself, say the other person's name first.

Example: John and I are students.

---

3. Listen: Miss Wilson and I are from the United States.
M1 We're from the USA.
We're instructors.
Rep: We're in the English class.
We're new students.
We're from Latin America.
We're from Asia.
We're confused.

4. (Singular and Plural *You*)
M2 T: Are you undergraduates or graduate students? S: We're (undergraduates).
Are you from the US or ( )? I'm from ( ).
Are you from ( ) or ( )?
Are you and ( ) from ( ) or ( )?
Am I from ( ) or the US?
Is ( ) from ( ) or ( )?
Are ( ) and ( ) from ( ) or ( )?
Are you a (biology) student or a (chemistry) student?
Am I a graduate student or a professor?

5. (Affirmative and Negative)
M2 T: Are you students? S: Yes, we are.
Are you undergraduates? (No, we aren't. We're graduate students.)
Are you from (Asia)?
Are you (biology) students?
Is ( ) from (Latin America)?
Is ( ) an undergraduate?
Is ( ) a (biologist)?
Are you a (math) student?
Are you (biologists)?
Are you from (Latin America)?
Is ( ) from the US?

6. T: Ask ( ) if he is from (Mexico). S1: Are you from Mexico?
C S2: (Yes, I am.)
(No, I'm not. I'm from (Japan)).
Ask ( ) if he is a (biologist). S1: Are you a biologist?
S2: (Yes, I am.)
Ask ( ) if he is from (China).
Ask ( ) if ( ) is from (Saudi Arabia).
Ask ( ) if she is an undergraduate.
Ask ( ) if ( ) and ( ) are graduate students.
Ask ( ) if he is a (chemistry) student.
Ask ( ) if ( ) and ( ) are from (Canada).
Ask ( ) if she is a graduate student.
Ask ( ) if he and ( ) are (math) students.
Ask ( ) if ( ) is from (Colombia).

SECTION TWO

Alternative Question

Chen: Is she a student or the teacher?
Nancy: Both.
Chen: What? I don't understand. Is she the professor or just a student?
Nancy: She's a TA, a graduate student.

Generalization

The word *or* is a conjunction. *It* indicates a choice.

Examples:

Is the professor tall or short?	She's tall.
Is Chen from Hong Kong or Taiwan?	He's from Taiwan.

---

1. Rep: Is the girl tall or short? — She's tall.
M1
Is she a student or the teacher? — She's a student.
Is the man old or young? — He's young.
Is he the lab assistant or the professor? — He's the lab assistant.
Is he fat or thin? — He's fat.
Is the woman a biologist or a chemist? — She's a biologist.
Is she tall or short? — She's tall.

2. Rep: Is the woman tall or short?
M1 Sub: fat or thin — S: Is the woman fat or thin?
a biologist or a chemist — Is the woman a biologist or a chemist?
a teaching assistant or a professor — Is the woman a teaching assistant or a professor?

3. Rep: Are the men graduate students or undergraduates?
M1 Sub: good students or bad students — S: Are the men good students or bad students?
from Asia or from Latin America — Are the men from Asia or from Latin America?
graduate students or undergraduates — Are the men graduate students or undergraduates?
in biology or chemistry — Are the men in biology or chemistry?

4. T: Ask about the woman. — S1: Is the woman tall or short?
M2 tall/short — S2: She's (tall).
T: Ask about the man. — S1: Is the man a student or a teacher?
student/teacher — S2: He's a (teacher) (student).

Exercise continues on next page.

T: Ask about the boys.
fat/thin
Ask about the woman.
lab assistant/teacher
Ask about the man.
tall/short
Ask about the men.
teaching assistants/teachers
Ask about the boys.
undergraduates/graduate students
Ask about the girl.
a biology student/a chemistry student
Ask about the boy.
handsome/ugly
Ask about the women.
biologists/chemists

5. C T: Ask a question about your classmate's country.
S1: Is ( ) big or small?
S2: It's small. (It's not big or small.)

Ask about ( )'s books.
S1: Are the books (expensive)?
S2: They're (cheap).

Ask about the capital of ( ).
Ask about the dorms.
Ask about the university buildings.
Ask about the weather in ( ).
Ask about cars in ( ).
Ask about universities in ( ).
Ask about ( )'s profession.
Ask about professors at ( ).
Ask about students in ( ).

6. C T: I think (Pablo) is from (Mexico).
S1: Is Pablo from Mexico?
S2: (Yes, he is.) (No, he isn't. He's from Venezuela. Carlos is from Mexico.)

T: I think (New York) is the capital of the US.
S1: Is New York the capital of the US?
S2: No, it isn't. Washington, D.C. is the capital.

I think ( ) is a biologist.
I think ( ) is a graduate student.
I think ( ) and ( ) are from ( ).
I think ( ) and ( ) are engineering students.
I think (city) is beautiful.
I think ( ) is from (city).

I think ( ) is the capital of ( ).
I think ( ) and ( ) are undergraduates.
I think ( ) is a chemist.
I think ( ) is from (Latin America).

SECTION THREE

Wh Questions

Generalization

The questions in Sections One and Two are answered by *yes* and *no*.
The questions in this section begin with a question word (*wh* word) and are answered differently.

Example: Carlos is from Latin America.

Wh Question: Who is from Latin America?

Answer: Carlos.

Example: The campus is confusing.

Wh Question: What is confusing?

Answer: The campus.

What question word asks about people? (*Who*)
What question word asks about things? (*What*)

Part A. *Who—What* in Subject Position

Carlos: Who's the professor?
Chen: The woman is. She's a TA.
Carlos: What's a TA?
Chen: I don't know.
Ali: That means *teaching assistant*.

1.	Rep:	Who is the professor?	The woman is.
M1		Who is the TA?	She is.
		Who is from Asia?	Chen is.
		Who is from Latin America?	Carlos is.
		What is a TA?	A teaching assistant.
		What is confusing?	The campus.
		What is easy?	The class.
		What is expensive?	The books.

Note: The answers to questions are often a subject and a verb or just a phrase. It is not usual in speaking to answer with a whole sentence.

2.	T:	He is tall.	S:	Who is tall?
M1		She is thin.		Who is thin?
		He is handsome.		Who is handsome?
		She is intelligent.		Who is intelligent?
		It is confusing.		What is confusing?
		It is expensive.		What is expensive?
		It is dirty.		What is dirty?
		It is tall.		What is tall?

3.	T:	He is fat.	S:	Who is fat?
M1T		It is clean.		What is clean?
		She is lost.		Who is lost?
		He is a biologist.		Who is a biologist?
		It is confusing.		What is confusing?
		It is cheap.		What is cheap?
		She is from the US.		Who is from the US?
		She is a TA.		Who is a TA?

4.	T:	He is from (Asia).	S1:	Who is from (Asia)?
M2			S2:	( ) is.
		It is expensive.	S1:	What is expensive?
			S2:	The (book) is.
		He is an undergraduate.		
		She is from (Latin America).		
		It is dirty.		
		She is a graduate student.		
		She is a (chemist).		
		He is a teacher.		
		It is tall.		
		He is intelligent.		
		She is confused.		

5. T: Ask (student) about the capital of the U.S. — S1: *What* is the capital of the U.S.?
C — S2: Washington, D.C.

Ask ( ) about the teacher. — S1: *Who* is the teacher?
S2: ( ) is.

Ask ( ) about the capital of ( ).
Ask ( ) about the (lab) teacher.
Ask ( ) about the textbook for this class.
Ask ( ) about ( ).

Part B. *Where?*

Chen: Are you from around here?
Ali: No.
Chen: Where are you from?
Ali: I'm from the Middle East. My name is Ali.
Chen: My name is Chen.
Carlos: I'm Carlos.
Ali: How long have you been here?
Carlos: Uh, not long.

Generalization

Where asks about a place.

Example: Are you from China?
Where are you from?

---

1. Rep: Where are you from?
M1 Where is he from?
Where is she from?
Where is it from?
Where are they from?

2. Rep: Where are you from?
M1T Sub: they — S: Where are they from?
he — Where is he from?
she — Where is she from?
it — Where is it from?
you — Where are you from?

3. T: Ask ( ) where he's from. — S1: Where are you from?
C — S2: I'm from (Saudi Arabia).

Ask ( ) where ( ) and ( ) are from. — S1: Where are ( ) and ( ) from?
S2: ( ) is from ( ); ( ) is from ( ).

Exercise continues on next page.

Ask ( ) where she's from.
Ask ( ) where the teacher is from.
Ask ( ) where ( ) is from.
Ask ( ) where he's from.
Ask ( ) where ( ) and ( ) are from.

SECTION FOUR

Alternative Negative Forms

Chen: Is the teaching assistant a professor?
Ali: She's not a professor. She's a graduate student in biology.
Carlos: Are you a graduate student?
Ali: No, I'm not. I'm a junior.

Generalization

Except for *I*, there are two forms of the negative contraction.

Examples:

I am not	=	I'm not		——
You are not	=	You're not	=	You aren't
He is not	=	He's not	=	He isn't
She is not	=	She's not	=	She isn't
It is not	=	It's not	=	It isn't
We are not	=	We're not	=	We aren't
They are not	=	They're not	=	They aren't

Both forms are very common. Practice the form which is easiest for you.

---

1. Rep: I'm not a student.
M1 Sub: We — S: We're not students.
He — He's not a student.
She — She's not a student.
They — They're not students.
You (Singular) — You're not a student.
You (Plural) — You're not students.
I — I'm not a student.

		T	S
2.	T:	He isn't tall.	S: He's not tall.
M1T		She isn't a professor.	She's not a professor.
		We aren't biologists.	We're not biologists.
		They aren't from Asia.	They're not from Asia.
		You aren't from the U.S.	You're not from the U.S.
		She isn't fat.	She's not fat.
		It isn't confusing.	It's not confusing.
		It isn't a classroom.	It's not a classroom.

		T	S
3.	T:	Am I a student?	S: No, you're not.
M1T		Are we in (New York)?	No, we're not.
		Is she from (Latin America)?	No, she's not.
		Are you TAs?	No, we're not.
		Are you (biologists)?	No, we're not.
		Is he from (Mexico)?	No, he's not.
		Are you from around here?	No, we're not.
		Are they undergraduates?	No, they're not.

SUMMARY DIALOGUE

First Day of Class

Note: Now listen to the dialogue to review Lesson One. The underlined words are emphasized more than the other words. Listen carefully.

Introduction

Carlos and Chen are students at a large American university. It is in a large city. They are foreign students. Carlos is from Latin America and Chen is from Asia. The campus is confusing and the boys are lost. All the buildings are gray.

1. Chen: Are the students here?

2. Carlos: No, the room isn't open. Maybe they're late.

3. Chen: Maybe they're lost.

4. Carlos: No, the students aren't lost.

5. Chen: Maybe the professor's lost.

6. Carlos: No . . . Here comes a student. Ask her.

7. Chen: You ask her.

8. Carlos: OK. Uh . . . Excuse me. I think I'm lost. Is this Allen Hall?

9. Nancy: Yeah. Are you in Biology 110?

10. Chen: Yes.

11. Nancy: Then you're not lost. This is it, room 232. Are you guys biology majors?

12. Chen: What?

13. Nancy: Are you from around here?

14. Carlos: No, I'm from Latin America.

15. Chen: And I'm from Asia.

16. Nancy: I'm from . . . Uh-oh, here's the teacher.

17. Chen: Is she the professor or a student?

18. Nancy: Both.

19. Carlos: I don't understand.

20. Nancy: She's a TA, a graduate student.

21. Chen: (to Carlos) Who's the professor?

22. Carlos: (pointing) She is. She's a TA.

23. Chen: What's a TA?

24. Carlos: I don't know.

25. Ali: (interrupts to explain) That means *teaching assistant*.

26. Chen: Oh . . . are you from around here?

27. Ali: No, I'm a foreign student, from the Middle East. My name's Ali. (He holds out his hand to shake hands.)

28. Chen: My name's Chen. (Shakes.)

29. Carlos: I'm Carlos. (Shakes.)

30. Ali: How long have you been in the U.S.?

31. Carlos: Uh . . . not long.

32. Chen: What's a teaching assistant?

33. Ali: The woman is a teacher, but not a professor. She's a graduate student in biology.

34. Carlos: Are you a graduate student?

35. Ali: No, I'm not. I'm a junior.

Communication Notes

1) Line 11. Guys—informal usage to address people of both sexes.

2) Line 11. Room numbers are pronounced in groups of two, if possible. Example: Room 232 (two, thirty-two); Room 1025 (ten, twenty-five). In tall buildings, the first number (or first two) indicates the floor. Room 232 is on what floor? Room 1025?

3) In the U.S., when people are introduced to others or introduce themselves, they shake hands and tell something about themselves. (See the dialogue.) Men always shake hands, but women sometimes do not. The custom varies; ask your teacher.

COMMUNICATIVE ACTIVITIES

1) Practice introductions. Your teacher will hand out cards of fictitious people like this:

Name: George Washington
Place: USA
Info: Graduate Student

Introduce yourself as the person on the card and find out who the other people are.

2) Practice Questions. Student 1 thinks of a famous person, place or thing.

Example: Paris. The other students ask questions answered by *yes* or *no*.

S2: Is it a man?	S1: No, it isn't.
S3: Is it a country?	S1: No, it isn't.
S4: Is it a city?	S1: Yes, it is.
S5: Is it in the US?	S1: No, it isn't.

Note to teacher: Students may be divided into teams for competition. Set a maximum number of questions before the game should end.

Lesson Two

In the Cafeteria

Introduction

After class Chen, Carlos, and Ali are in the cafeteria. They are having coffee. It's very crowded. Everyone is starting classes today. Chen is studying biology. Carlos is taking biology and chemistry. Both are studying English, too. Ali is a chemistry major. He's taking one biology course. All three are talking about the first day of classes.

Comprehension Questions

1. Who's in the cafeteria?
2. What are they doing?
3. What is Chen taking?
4. What are both Carlos and Chen studying?
5. What's Ali's major?
6. What are they talking about?

Vocabulary

Nouns

biology
breakfast
chemistry
class
coffee
computer science
dinner
engineering
language lab
lunch
major
movies
park
school
tea

Verbs

belong to
do
eat
forget
go
have
leave
live
start
stay
study
teach
take
talk

Adverbs

both
downtown
somewhere
today
tomorrow
tonight

Adjective

crowded

Pronouns

someone
something

SECTION ONE

Present Continuous

Part A. Affirmative

Carlos: I'm staying with a family.
Ali: How's it going? Are you learning much English?
Carlos: No, I'm not. But they're learning a lot of Spanish. How about you?
Chen: I'm living in the dorms. They're awful.

Generalization

This verb tense (BE + verb-*ing*) is called Present Continuous. It indicates that the action is happening right now, or will happen in the near future. Note that the BE forms are the same as in Lesson One:

Lesson One: The boy *is* in the room. (BE—Simple Present)

Lesson Two: The boy *is studying* in the room. (Present Continuous)

---

1. Rep: The boys are having coffee.
M1
Everyone is starting classes today.
Chen is studying biology.
Both boys are taking English.
They are talking to Ali.
Carlos is staying with a family.
Chen is living in the dorms.
They are having a good time.

2. Rep: The man is learning biology now.
M1 Sub:

Sub	S
taking	The man is taking biology now.
studying	The man is studying biology now.
teaching	The man is teaching biology now.
starting	The man is starting biology now.
learning	The man is learning biology now.

3. Rep: The women are studying computer science.
M1 Sub:

Sub	S
learning	The women are learning computer science.
teaching	The women are teaching computer science.
taking	The women are taking computer science.
starting	The women are starting computer science.
studying	The women are studying computer science.

4.	Rep:	I'm having coffee at the cafeteria today.		
M1	Sub:	lunch	S:	I'm having lunch at the cafeteria today.
		tea		I'm having tea at the cafeteria today.
		dinner		I'm having dinner at the cafeteria today.
		breakfast		I'm having breakfast at the cafeteria today.
		lunch		I'm having lunch at the cafeteria today.
		coffee		I'm having coffee at the cafeteria today.

5.	Rep:	The boys are taking the biology class.		
M1T	Sub:	the girl	S:	The girl is taking the biology class.
		I		I am taking the biology class.
		the boy		The boy is taking the biology class.
		we		We are taking the biology class.
		you		You are taking the biology class.
		the man		The man is taking the biology class.

Note: Place Expressions

The girls are going to the cafeteria.
to the movies.
to school.
to class.
home.
downtown.

Some place expressions are preceded by *to the;* some by *to;* others by no preposition. Learn the expressions in sentences.

6.	Rep:	The boys are going to the movies.		
M1	Sub:	to the cafeteria	S:	The boys are going to the cafeteria.
		to school		The boys are going to school.
		home		The boys are going home.
		to the dorm		The boys are going to the dorm.
		to class		The boys are going to class.
		downtown		The boys are going downtown.
		to biology class		The boys are going to biology class.
		to the movies		The boys are going to the movies.

7.	Rep:	The girl is going downtown.		
M1T	Sub:	home	S:	The girl is going home.
		girls		The girls are going home.
		to school		The girls are going to school.
		boys		The boys are going to school.
		downtown		The boys are going downtown.
		boy		The boy is going downtown.

		to class	The boy is going to class.
		you	You are going to class.
		to the movies	You are going to the movies.
		I	I am going to the movies.

8. T: Are you studying English or biology? S: I'm studying English.
M2 Is ( ) going home or to class? (She)'s going to class.
Are ( ) and ( ) eating at the cafeteria or at home?
Are you eating at home or at the cafeteria?
Is ( ) having breakfast or lunch?
Am I having coffee or tea?
Are ( ) and ( ) going to the cafeteria or the language lab?
Are you going downtown or to class?
Is ( ) going home or to the language lab?
Are ( ) and ( ) going to class or to the park?
Is ( ) taking biology or chemistry?
Are you studying engineering or computer science?
Are we studying English or (Chinese)?

9. T: What are you studying? S: I'm studying (engineering).
C Where is ( ) studying? (He)'s studying (at the university).
Where are you studying?
What is ( ) studying?
Who is teaching?
Where are you going for lunch?
Where is ( ) having lunch?
What are you having for lunch?
Where are you having dinner?
Where are you living now?
Where are ( ) and ( ) staying?

Part B. Question and Short Answer

Vocabulary

Verbs	*Adverbs*
come	this afternoon
drink	tomorrow
eat	tonight
play	
walk	

Ali: Are you going to class this afternoon?
Chen: Yes, we are. We're taking an English course.
Carlos: Are you studying English now?
Ali: No, I'm free this afternoon. I'm playing soccer with some friends.
Chen: What's "soccer"?
Ali: You know, football.

Generalization

Lesson One:	The woman [is] a biologist.	
	[Is] the woman a biologist?	Yes, she is. (No, she isn't.)
Lesson Two:	The girl [is] taking English.	
	[Is] the girl taking English?	No, she isn't. (Yes, she is.)

Note: The Present Continuous may refer to the near future:

"Are you playing soccer tonight?"

The time word *tonight* asks about the future.

---

1. Rep: Are the boys going to class?
M1
Is Carlos taking English?
Is he having coffee?
Is Ali going downtown?
Are they studying English?
Is Chen playing soccer?
Are we having lunch?

2. **M1**

T:	S:
The girl is having coffee.	Is the girl having coffee?
The boy is eating dinner.	Is the boy eating dinner?
The student is drinking tea.	Is the student drinking tea?
The man is having lunch.	Is the man having lunch?
The instructor is eating breakfast.	Is the instructor eating breakfast?
The woman is drinking coffee.	Is the woman drinking coffee?
The teacher is having dinner.	Is the teacher having dinner?

3. **M1**

T:	S:
The men are walking to class.	Are the men walking to class?
The teachers are going home.	Are the teachers going home?
The girls are going downtown.	Are the girls going downtown?
The boys are playing soccer.	Are the boys playing soccer?
We're going downtown this afternoon.	Are we going downtown this afternoon?

	You're playing soccer tomorrow.		Are you playing soccer tomorrow?
	We're taking an English course.		Are we taking an English course?
	They're walking to class today.		Are they walking to class today?

4.	T:	The boys are taking English.	S:	Are the boys taking English?
M1T		The girl is studying engineering.		Is the girl studying engineering?
		The women are learning (Spanish).		Are the women learning Spanish?
		The instructor is teaching biology.		Is the instructor teaching biology?
		The girls are going to chemistry class.		Are the girls going to chemistry class?
		She's taking chemistry.		Is she taking chemistry?
		We're studying biology.		Are we studying biology?
		You're learning English.		Are you learning English?
		They're teaching computer science.		Are they teaching computer science?
		The women are taking chemistry.		Are the women taking chemistry?
		The boys are going to the language lab.		Are the boys going to the language lab?
		The man is learning Chinese.		Is the man learning Chinese?
		She is studying computer science.		Is she studying computer science?
		They are teaching this afternoon.		Are they teaching this afternoon?

Generalization

The short answers are the same as in Lesson One (see Exercise 5).

5.	Listen:	Is the girl taking biology?	Yes, she is.
M1		Is she taking physics?	No, she isn't.
		Are the teachers going home?	Yes, they are.
		Are they going downtown?	No, they aren't.

6.	T:	Is (teacher) teaching the class?	S:	Yes, (he) is.
M2		Is (teacher) taking the class?		No, (he) isn't.
		Is ( ) studying computer science?		
		Are you taking biology?		
		Is ( ) taking biology?		
		Are ( ) and ( ) learning Spanish?		
		Is ( ) studying chemistry?		
		Are you walking home this afternoon?		
		Is ( ) going to (New York) tonight?		
		Are ( ) and ( ) going downtown this afternoon?		
		Is ( ) playing soccer tomorrow?		
		Are you staying with a family?		
		Is ( ) living in the dorm?		
		Are ( ) and ( ) living downtown?		

7. Ask your classmates. Ask a classmate about the things you are studying in this chapter. Then tell your other classmates.

Example:

You:	Are you living in the dorm?
Classmate:	No, I'm not. I'm staying with a family.
You:	( ) is staying with a family.

Part C. Negative

Vocabulary

Verbs	*Nouns*
come	library
drive	math (mathematics)
read	someone
tell	something
work	somewhere

Nancy: Hi, Chen. Are you enjoying the food here?
Chen: What food?
Ali: We aren't having lunch. Just coffee.

Note: Remember there are two ways to form the negative (except for first person singular.*)

You aren't	=	You're not
He isn't	=	He's not
She isn't	=	She's not
It isn't	=	It's not
We aren't	=	We're not
They aren't	=	They're not

*For first person singular there's only one negative: I'm not.

1. Rep: I'm not learning English.
M1
He isn't learning French.
You aren't teaching biology.
The girl isn't living in the dorm.
We aren't going downtown.
The boys aren't playing soccer.
She isn't staying at home.

2. T: They're having dinner at home. S: They aren't having dinner at home.
M1T
We're going to the movies. — We aren't going to the movies.
The girls are walking home. — The girls aren't walking home.
They're staying with a family. — They aren't staying with a family.
The girl is learning Spanish. — The girl isn't learning Spanish.
The boys are studying biology. — The boys aren't studying biology.
He's taking computer science. — He isn't taking computer science.

3. Rep: He's not learning English.
M1
The girl's not learning English.
The boy's not studying English.
We're not studying biology.
You're not studying biology.
They're not going downtown.

4. T: He isn't studying engineering. S: He's not studying engineering.
M1
We aren't going to the movies. — We're not going to the movies.
They aren't walking home. — They're not walking home.
She isn't going to class. — She's not going to class.
You aren't taking chemistry. — You're not taking chemistry.
They boy isn't staying with a family. — The boy's not staying with a family.

5. Erroneous Statements
M2 T: live in the dorm
S1: ( ) is living in the dorm.
S2: I'm not living in the dorm.
(I'm living with a family.)

study chemistry
S1: ( ) is studying chemistry.
S2: I'm not studying chemistry.
(I'm studying biology.)

learn Spanish
have lunch in the cafeteria
walk downtown
teach English
play soccer
go to the movies
take computer science
drive home
walk to the language lab
study engineering

6. T: Tell something you're doing now. S: (I'm studying English now.)
C Tell something you're not doing now. (I'm not playing soccer.)
Tell something ( ) is doing now.
Tell something ( ) and ( ) are doing now.
Tell something ( ) is not doing.
Tell something ( ) and ( ) are not doing.

7. Ask your classmates.* Find out where your neighbor is going for (lunch) today and
C tell the teacher.

Example:
S1: Are you going to the cafeteria for lunch today?
S2: (No, I'm going home.)
S1: (He's) going home for lunch today.

SECTION TWO

Wh Questions

Vocabulary

Nouns	*Verbs*	*Indefinites*
cook	cook	some
kitchen	do	someone
letter	read	something
park	work	somewhere
	write	

Adverb	*Expression*
just	well then

Nancy: Where are you going?
Ali: To Alder Park. I'm playing soccer this afternoon.
Carlos: What are you doing this afternoon, Nancy?
Nancy: Working in the kitchen. I'm a cook.
Chen: Well then, who's going to English class?
Nancy: Not me.
Carlos: Not me. I'm writing a letter.

*Everyone should have a chance to ask questions and report.

Part A. *Who?*

1. Rep: Who's going to class?
M1
Who's studying this afternoon?
Who's having coffee at the cafeteria?
Who's going to Alder Park?
Who's working in the kitchen?

Generalization

The question word *who* used as subject in the Present Continuous is followed by the singular *is*. The answer may be singular or plural.

Examples:

Who is studying?	Chen is.
Who is studying?	Chen and Carlos are.

---

2. **M1**

T:	S:
Someone's studying.	Who's studying?
Someone's going to class.	Who's going to class?
Someone's having coffee.	Who's having coffee?
Someone's playing soccer.	Who's playing soccer?
Some people are having lunch.	Who's having lunch?
Some people are studying.	Who's studying?
Some people are working in the kitchen.	Who's working in the kitchen?
Some people are walking to class.	Who's walking to class?

3. **M1T**

T: going to class/Carlos and Chen
S1: Who's going to class?
S2: Carlos and Chen are.

having coffee in the cafeteria/the boys
S1: Who's having coffee in the cafeteria?
S2: The boys are.

walking to class/Chen and Carlos
studying English/the boys
taking biology/the students
learning English/Carlos and Chen
going to class this afternoon/the boys

4. **M2**

T: Ask ( ) who is studying (biology).
S1: Who's studying biology?
S2: ( ) and ( ) are.

Ask ( ) who is walking home today.
Ask ( ) who is having lunch at the cafeteria.
Ask ( ) who is taking (math).
Ask ( ) who is learning (Spanish).
Ask ( ) who is going downtown today.

Exercise continues on next page.

Ask ( ) who is walking to the park this afternoon.
Ask ( ) who is going to the movies tonight.
Ask ( ) who is playing soccer in the park.
Ask ( ) who is eating lunch at the cafeteria tomorrow.
Ask ( ) who is having dinner at home tonight.
Ask ( ) who is going to the cafeteria for coffee.

Part B. *What?*

Generalization

Yes/No Question: Is Ali studying engineering?
Wh Question: What is Ali studying? Answer: Chemistry.

---

1. Rep: What is Chen studying?
M1 Sub: learning — S: What is Chen learning?
writing — What is Chen writing?
taking — What is Chen taking?
playing — What is Chen playing?
doing — What is Chen doing?
reading — What is Chen reading?
studying — What is Chen studying?

2. Rep: What are Carlos and Chen doing?
M1 Sub: studying — S: What are Carlos and Chen studying?
the boys — What are the boys studying?
Ali — What is Ali studying?
taking — What is Ali taking?
Carlos — What is Carlos taking?
doing — What is Carlos doing?
Chen and Carlos — What are Chen and Carlos doing?

3. T: Is Chen doing something? — S: What is Chen doing?
M1 Are the boys learning something? — What are the boys learning?
Is Nancy studying something? — What is Nancy studying?
Are Carlos and Chen taking something? — What are Carlos and Chen taking?
Is Chen writing something? — What is Chen writing?
Is Ali playing something? — What is Ali playing?
Is Nancy cooking something? — What is Nancy cooking?

4. T: Someone is studying. S: Who is studying?
M1T
He is doing something. — What is he doing?
Some people are working. — Who is working?
She is reading something. — What is she reading?
Someone is cooking. — Who is cooking?
Someone is writing. — Who is writing?
He is writing something. — What is he writing?
She is reading something. — What is she reading?
Some people are playing. — Who is playing?
Someone is reading. — Who is reading?

Note: In conversation, the answer to a *wh* question can be short.
A: What are you doing? B: Writing a letter.
A: What are you writing? B: A letter.

---

5. T: Someone is reading.
M2
S1: Who is reading?
S2: (   ) is.
S1: What is (   ) reading?
S2: (A book.)

Some people are studying.
S1: Who is studying?
S2: (   ) and (   ) are.
S1: What are they studying?
S2: (Biology.)

Someone is teaching.
Some people are cooking.
Someone is playing.
Some people are learning.
Someone is writing.
Some people are reading.
Someone is studying.
Some people are working.

6. Find out what your classmates are doing this afternoon. Report to the class.
C
Example: S1: What are you doing this afternoon? S2: (I'm going home.)
S1: She's going home.

Example: S1: What are you studying this afternoon? S2: I'm studying (English).
S1: He's studying English.

Part C. *Where?*

Chen: Where are you going now?
Ali: To the cafeteria for coffee.

1.	Rep:	Where are you going now?	
M1	Sub:	Ali	S: Where is Ali going now?
		the boys	Where are the boys going now?
		Nancy	Where is Nancy going now?
		Chen and Carlos	Where are Chen and Carlos going now?
		the student	Where is the student going now?
		we	Where are we going now?
		you	Where are you going now?
		she	Where is she going now?

2.	T:	Is Ali going somewhere?	S: Where is Ali going?
M1T		Are the boys doing something?	What are the boys doing?
		Is Nancy walking somewhere?	Where is Nancy walking?
		Is Chen going somewhere?	Where is Chen going?
		Is Carlos reading something?	What is Carlos reading?
		Is she working somewhere?	Where is she working?
		Are they learning something?	What are they learning?
		Is he playing somewhere?	Where is he playing?
		Are they cooking something?	What are they cooking?

3.	T:	Nancy is working somewhere.	S1: Where is Nancy working?
M2			S2: (In the cafeteria.)
		The boys are learning something.	S1: What are the boys learning?
			S2: (English.)
		Someone is having coffee.	S1: Who is having coffee?
			S2: (Carlos.)
		The man is teaching something.	
		Carlos and Chen are reading something.	
		Someone is playing soccer.	
		Chen is going somewhere.	
		Someone is having coffee.	
		The boy is cooking something.	
		They are having coffee somewhere.	
		Someone is writing a letter.	
		We are playing soccer somewhere.	

4. Ask your classmates. Find out what your neighbor is doing this
C afternoon and tell the class.

Example:
S1: What are you doing this afternoon?
S2: (Playing soccer.)
S1: Where are you playing?
S2: (In the park.)
S1: ( ) is playing soccer in the park this afternoon.

SECTION THREE

Possessive

Vocabulary

Nouns	*Verbs*	*Possessive Pronoun*
bag	belong to	whose
job	know	
model	look at	*Adverb*
newspaper	think	probably
notebook		
pen		

Carlos: Look at that on the table!
Chen: I think its Ali's watch. He probably forgot it.
Nancy: No, I know it's not Ali's.
Carlos: Whose is it then?
Nancy: The boss's.
Chen: What?
Nancy: It belongs to the boss.

Part A. Names

Generalization

In spelling, add *'s* to names to show possession.

Example:
The watch belongs to Ali. It's Ali's watch.

1.
M1

Listen:	Rep:
Whose watch is that?	It's Ali's watch.
Whose book is that?	It's Chen's book.
Whose pen is that?	It's Nancy's pen.
Whose notebook is that?	It's Mohammed's notebook.
Whose bag is that?	It's Maria's bag.
Whose newspaper is that?	It's Jack's newspaper.

2. T: pen—Nancy S: It's Nancy's pen.
M1

T:	S:
pen—Nancy	It's Nancy's pen.
watch—Ali	It's Ali's watch.
notebook—Chen	It's Chen's notebook.
book—Maria	It's Maria's book.
newspaper—Jack	It's Jack's newspaper.
bag—Hassan	It's Hassan's bag.
coffee—Bob	It's Bob's coffee.
tea—Pat	It's Pat's tea.
breakfast—Mohammed	It's Mohammed's breakfast.
dinner—Pablo	It's Pablo's dinner.

Generalization

When the spelling of a name ends in *s* or *z*, some people pronounce the possessive like this:

It's Mr. Jone*s's* book	[ziz]
It's Dori*s's* book	[siz]

Some people pronounce the possessive like this:

It's Mr. Jone*s'* book.	[z]
It's Dori*s'* paper.	[s]

3.
M1

T:	S:
The book belongs to Mr. Jones.	It's Mr. Jones' book.
The paper belongs to Doris.	It's Doris' paper.
The pen belongs to Carlos.	It's Carlos' pen.
The watch belongs to Luis.	It's Luis' watch.
The notebook belongs to Gladys.	It's Gladys' notebook.
The book belongs to Dr. Harris.	It's Dr. Harris' book.
The paper belongs to Lois.	It's Lois' paper.

4. Negative Answer
M2 T: book—(Maria)

S1: Is it Maria's book?
S2: No, it isn't. It's (Carlos's) book.

pen—(Ali)
notebook—( )
watch—( )
paper—( )
bag—( )
coffee—( )
tea—( )
dinner—( )
breakfast—( )

Part B. Nouns

5. Listen: Whose watch is this? Rep: It's the boy's watch.
M1
Whose pen is this? — It's the student's pen.
Whose book is this? — It's the girl's book.
Whose notebook is this? — It's the woman's notebook.
Whose paper is this? — It's the man's paper.
Whose coffee is this? — It's the boys' coffee.
Whose breakfast is this? — It's the man's breakfast.
Whose tea is this? — It's the woman's tea.

Note: In speech there is no difference in sound between the singular and plural possessives of regular nouns:

The boy's book. (1 boy, 1 book)
The boys' book. (several boys, 1 book)

In writing, add ' if the noun ends in *-s;* add *'s* if it does not.

---

6. T: The book belongs to the boy. S: It's the boy's book.
M1T
The book belongs to the boys. — It's the boys' book.
The pen belongs to the teacher. — It's the teacher's pen.
The watch belongs to the girl. — It's the girl's watch.
The bag belongs to the woman. — It's the woman's bag.
The book belongs to the students. — It's the students' book.

7. Rep: I'm reading Chen's book.
M1T T: Ali S: I'm reading Ali's book.
Carlos
Nancy
the boys
the teacher
the cook
the women
the girls

8. Objects in the Classroom
M2 T: Whose book is this? S: It's (Jose)'s book.
Whose pen is this?
Whose paper is this?
Whose notebook is this?
Whose bag is this?
Whose watch is this?
etc.

9. In some countries, jobs are for men or women.
C T: Find out about these jobs in your friends' countries.

Example: 1) doctor

S1: Is a doctor's job a man's or a woman's job?
S2: (It's a woman's job in my country.)
(Both men and women are doctors.)

2) teacher
3) nurse
4) engineer
5) cook
etc.

SUMMARY DIALOGUE

Talking in the Cafeteria

1. Carlos: I'm staying with a family now.

2. Ali: How's it going? Are you learning much English?

3. Carlos: No. But they're learning Spanish. How about you?

4. Chen: I'm living in the dorms. They're awful.

5. Ali: Say, are you two busy this afternoon?

6. Chen: Yes, we're taking an English course.

7. Ali: Too bad. I'm playing soccer with some friends. Are you soccer players?

8. Chen: What's "soccer"?

9. Ali: You know, football.

10. Chen: Oh, I see.

11. Nancy: Hi, Chen. Are you enjoying the food?

12. Chen: Food?

13. Ali: We aren't having lunch. Just coffee. Here, take my seat, Nancy. I'm leaving.

14. Nancy: Where are you going?

15. Ali: To Alder Park. I'm playing soccer this afternoon. (He leaves.)

16. Nancy: You're lucky. Have fun.

17. Carlos: What are you doing this afternoon, Nancy?

18. Nancy: Working in the kitchen. I'm a cook. Are you guys staying for lunch?

19. Carlos: Look at that, on the seat there. What is it?

20. Chen: I think it's Ali's watch. He probably forgot it.

21. Nancy: No, I know it's not Ali's.

22. Carlos: Whose is it then?

23. Nancy: The boss's.

24. Carlos: Sorry?

25. Nancy: It belongs to the boss. He's so forgetful.

Communication Notes

Line 24. Sorry? What does he mean?
Line 18. Who answers Nancy's question? Why?

COMMUNICATIVE ACTIVITIES

1) Greeting an Old Friend

Listen carefully as your teacher reads these short dialogues. Notice which words are stressed.

A) A: How are you?
B: Fine, thanks. And you?
A: Good, thanks. (What are you doing now?)

B) A: How are you?
B: Very good, thanks. How are you?
A: Fine. (Where are you working now?)

Use the Present Continuous to get information about your friend. Practice these greetings with a classmate.

2) Practice.

"We're going on a long trip next week. We're packing many things in the suitcase." The teacher begins: I'm packing (shoes). Students continue adding items in order, reciting the whole list each time.

Lesson Three

Taking the Bus

Introduction

It's Friday night. Saturday morning, Chen and Carlos are going to take the bus downtown. Carlos is going to buy a new camera. Chen isn't going to buy anything, but he's probably going to look at typewriters.

Vocabulary

Nouns		*Verbs*	*Indefinites*
bus stop	Saturday	buy	anything
camera	shirt	drive	
car	store	look at	
coat	taxi	travel	
dress	TV		
Friday	typewriter		
radio			

SECTION ONE

Going to (Future)

Part A-1. Affirmative

Generalization

The *going to* (Future) always indicates a future time. In Lesson Two the Present Continuous indicates present or future time, but has a time word to indicate the future.

Lesson Two	The boys are		playing soccer tomorrow.

Present Continuous
BE + verb + *ing*

Lesson Three	The boys are	going to	play soccer (tomorrow).

going to (future)
BE + *going to* + verb

---

1. Listen: I'm studying English now.
M1 I'm going to take Chinese next month.
I'm living in the dorm now.
I'm going to live with a family next year.

Rep: I'm going to take the bus downtown.
I'm going to buy a camera.
The boys are going to look at typewriters.
They're going to walk to the bus stop.
I'm going to take a taxi.
We're going to drive the car.

2. Rep: I'm going to buy a new camera.
M1

Sub:	S:
typewriter	I'm going to buy a new typewriter.
pen	I'm going to buy a new pen.
book	I'm going to buy a new book.
radio	I'm going to buy a new radio.
TV	I'm going to buy a new TV.
coat	I'm going to buy a new coat.
dress	I'm going to buy a new dress.

3. Rep: He's going to walk downtown.
M1

Sub:	S:
drive	He's going to drive downtown.
home	He's going to drive home.
take a bus	He's going to take a bus home.
to school	He's going to take a bus to school.
walk	He's going to walk to school.
to the park	He's going to walk to the park.
drive	He's going to drive to the park.
to town	He's going to drive to town.

4. Rep: I'm going to look at typewriters.
M1T

Sub:	S:
he	He's going to look at typewriters.
she	She's going to look at typewriters.
they	They're going to look at typewriters.
we	We're going to look at typewriters.

Exercise continues on next page.

	you	You're going to look at typewriters.
	I	I'm going to look at typewriters.

5. Rep: He's going to buy a new car.

M1T Sub:	radio	S: He's going to buy a new radio.
	look at	He's going to look at a new radio.
	I	I'm going to look at a new radio.
	typewriter	I'm going to look at a new typewriter.
	buy	I'm going to buy a new typewriter.
	you	You're going to buy a new typewriter.
	coat	You're going to buy a new coat.
	she	She's going to buy a new coat.

6. Chain Exercise
M2 The store is having a sale.
T: What are you going to buy?

S1: I'm going to buy a (coat).
S2: I'm going to buy a coat and a typewriter).
S3: I'm going to buy a coat and a typewriter and a (camera).

7. Chain Exercise
M2 You are going to travel.
T: Where are you going to travel?

S1: I'm going to travel to (Mexico).
S2: I'm going to travel to Mexico and (New York).
S3: I'm going to travel to Mexico and New York and (Cairo).

Part A-2. Interrogative

Carlos: Are you going to buy anything tomorrow?
Chen: No, I'm not.

Generalization

Lesson One:		The man [is]	a professor.	
	[Is]	the man	a professor?	Yes, he is. (No, he isn't.)
Lesson Two:		The man [is]	walking downtown.	
	[Is]	the man	walking downtown?	Yes, he is. (No, he isn't.)
Lesson Three:		The man [is]	going to walk downtown.	
	[Is]	the man	going to walk downtown?	Yes, he is. (No, he isn't.)

---

1. **M1** Listen: Carlos is going to buy a new camera.
Is Carlos going to buy a new camera?

The boys are going to walk downtown.
Are the boys going to walk downtown?

2. **M1T** Rep: Is Carlos going to buy a new camera?

Sub:	S:
coat	Is Carlos going to buy a new coat?
Nancy	Is Nancy going to buy a new coat?
typewriter	Is Nancy going to buy a new typewriter?
the boys	Are the boys going to buy a new typewriter?
TV	Are the boys going to buy a new TV?
the girl	Is the girl going to buy a new TV?
dress	Is the girl going to buy a new dress?

3. **M1T**

T:	S:
Carlos is going to buy a new camera.	Is Carlos going to buy a new camera?
The boys are going to take the bus.	Are the boys going to take the bus?
The girl is going to look at typewriters.	Is the girl going to look at typewriters?
We're going to take the bus downtown.	Are we going to take the bus downtown?
He's going to buy a new radio.	Is he going to buy a new radio?
They're going to travel to New York.	Are they going to travel to New York?
She's going to drive to the park.	Is she going to drive to the park?
Carlos and Chen are going to walk to the bus stop.	Are Carlos and Chen going to walk to the bus stop?

Part A-3. Negative

Carlos: How about a new typewriter?
Chen: No. I'm not going to buy a typewriter.

Generalization

The negative of the *going to* (future) is formed the same way as the negative in Lessons One and Two.

Examples:
I'm not going to travel to California.
He isn't going to buy a new camera. or
He's not going to buy a new camera.

---

4. **M1** Rep: I'm not going to buy a typewriter.

Sub:	S:
camera	I'm not going to buy a camera.
radio	I'm not going to buy a radio.
TV	I'm not going to buy a TV.

coat — I'm not going to buy a coat.
shirt — I'm not going to buy a shirt.
dress — I'm not going to buy a dress.

5. Alternative Negative Forms.
M1 Rep: I'm not going to buy a camera.

Sub: he — S: He's not going to buy a camera.
they — They're not going to buy a camera.
you — You're not going to buy a camera.
she — She's not going to buy a camera.
we — We're not going to buy a camera.

6. Negative Response
C T: Ask ( ) if she's going to buy a new coat.
S1: Are you going to buy a new coat?
S2: (No, I'm not. I'm going to buy a new dress.)

T: Ask ( ) if he and ( ) are going to travel to Venezuela.
S1: Are you and ( ) going to travel to Venezuela?
S2: (No, we aren't. We're going to travel to Japan.)

Ask ( ) if she's going to take the bus downtown.
Ask ( ) if she and ( ) are going to buy a TV.
Ask ( ) if he is going to have lunch downtown.
Ask ( ) if he and ( ) are going to buy a (car).
Ask ( ) if she's going to drive to (New York).
Ask ( ) if he is going to study (engineering).
Ask ( ) if she is going to take (Spanish).
Ask ( ) if he and ( ) are going to play soccer today.
Ask ( ) if she and ( ) are going to write letters this afternoon.
Ask ( ) if he is going to take a bus downtown tomorrow.

Part B. *Wh* Questions

Carlos: Well, what are you going to buy?
Chen: Lunch.

Generalization

Is Chen going to buy [something]?

[What] is Chen going to buy? Answer: Lunch.

---

1. Rep: What is the girl going to buy?
M1 Sub: do — S: What is the girl going to do?
study — What is the girl going to study?
cook — What is the girl going to cook?
eat — What is the girl going to eat?
buy — What is the girl going to buy?

2. Rep: What are the boys going to study?
M1 Sub: you — S: What are you going to study?
buy — What are you going to buy?
the girl — What is the girl going to buy?
study — What is the girl going to study?
the men — What are the men going to study?

3. T: Is Nancy going to buy something? — S: What is she going to buy?
M1T Are the boys going to do something? — What are they going to do?
Is Ali going to look at something? — What is he going to look at?
Are the women going to eat something? — What are they going to eat?
Is Chen going to cook something? — What is he going to cook?
Are the boys going to study something? — What are they going to study?
Are the students going to buy something? — What are they going to buy?

4. T: Ask ( ) what s/he's going to study. — S1: What are you going to study?
M2 S2: I'm going to study (computer science).

Ask ( ) what s/he's going to buy in town.
Ask ( ) what s/he's going to have for dinner tonight.
Ask ( ) what s/he's going to do this weekend.
Ask ( ) what s/he's going to write today.
Ask ( ) what s/he's going to read tonight.
Ask ( ) what s/he's going to cook for dinner.
Ask ( ) what s/he's going to have for lunch today.
Ask ( ) what s/he's going to do next weekend.

Note: *Where*

Is Chen going to travel [someplace]?

[Where] is Chen going to travel? Answer: To New York.

---

5. T: Chen is going to travel someplace. — S: Where is Chen going to travel?
M1 He's going to buy a new coat someplace. — Where is he going to buy a new coat?
The boys are going to have dinner someplace. — Where are the boys going to have dinner?
Nancy is going to eat lunch someplace. — Where is Nancy going to eat lunch.

She's going to look at books someplace. — Where is she going to look at books?
Carlos and Chen are going to have coffee someplace. — Where are Carlos and Chen going to have coffee?
They're going to buy a book someplace. — Where are they going to buy a book?

6. T: Chen is going to do something. — S: What is he going to do?
M1T Chen is going to study someplace. — Where is he going to study?
The boys are going to travel someplace. — Where are they going to travel?
The girls are going to buy something. — What are they going to buy?
The man is going to cook something. — What is he going to cook?
The women are going to have lunch someplace. — Where are they going to have lunch?
They're going to buy something. — What are they going to buy?
Chen and Carlos are going to have coffee someplace. — Where are they going to have coffee?

7. T: Ask ( ) where he's going to have dinner. — S1: Where are you going to have dinner?
M2 S2: I'm going to have dinner (at home).
Ask ( ) where he's going to study.
Ask ( ) where he's going to travel.
Ask ( ) where he's going to buy a camera.
Ask ( ) where he's going to have coffee.
Ask ( ) where he's going to have lunch.
Ask ( ) where he's going to study next year.
Ask ( ) where he's going to buy a new coat.
Ask ( ) where he's going to play soccer.
Ask ( ) where he's going to live next year.
Ask ( ) where he's going to travel next month.

Note: When

Is Chen going to buy a camera [sometime]?

[When] is Chen going to buy a camera? Answer: Tomorrow.

---

8. Rep: When is Carlos going to buy a camera?
M1 Sub: a typewriter — S: When is Carlos going to buy a typewriter?
Chen — When is Chen going to buy a typewriter?
a new camera — When is Chen going to buy a new camera?
the boys — When are the boys going to buy a new camera?
Nancy — When is Nancy going to buy a new camera?
a new TV — When is Nancy going to buy a new TV?

		Chen and Carlos		When are Chen and Carlos going to buy a new TV?
		a car		When are Chen and Carlos going to buy a car?
		the girl		When is the girl going to buy a car?

9.	T:	Chen and Ali are going to buy something.	S:	What are they going to buy?
M1T		The boys are going to look at typewriters sometime.		When are they going to look at typewriters?
		The boys are going to take the bus someplace.		Where are they going to take the bus?
		Chen is going to study sometime.		When is he going to study?
		Chen is going to study something.		What is he going to study?
		Nancy is going to eat lunch sometime.		When is she going to eat lunch?
		Nancy is going to eat lunch someplace.		Where is she going to eat?
		Nancy is going to eat something.		What is she going to eat?

10. Expressions of Future Time

M1	Rep:	I'm going to drive to Chicago next week.		
	Sub:	month	S:	I'm going to drive to Chicago next month.
		weekend		I'm going to drive to Chicago next weekend.
		Friday		I'm going to drive to Chicago next Friday.
		summer		I'm going to drive to Chicago next summer.
		year		I'm going to drive to Chicago next year.
		September		I'm going to drive to Chicago next September.
		Saturday		I'm going to drive to Chicago next Saturday.
		week		I'm going to drive to Chicago next week.

11.	Rep:	He's going to buy a camera tomorrow.		
M1	Sub:	this afternoon	S:	He's going to buy a camera this afternoon.
		tonight		He's going to buy a camera tonight.
		today		He's going to buy a camera today.
		this week		He's going to buy a camera this week.
		this weekend		He's going to buy a camera this weekend.
		this month		He's going to buy a camera this month.
		this year		He's going to buy a camera this year.
		tomorrow		He's going to buy a camera tomorrow.

12. Affirmative Answers

M2	T:	Ask ( ) if he's going to buy a car.	S1:	Are you going to buy a new car?
			S2:	Yes, I am.
		Ask when.	S1:	When are you going to buy a new car?
			S2:	I'm going to buy a new car (next year).
		Ask ( ) if he's going to drive downtown.		
		Ask ( ) if he's going to travel to (Canada).		
		Ask ( ) if she's going to take the bus (downtown).		
		Ask ( ) if he's going to buy a (camera).		

Exercise continues on next page.

Ask ( ) if she's going to look at new (TVs).
Ask ( ) if he's going to have (lunch).
Ask ( ) if she's going to study.
Ask ( ) if he's going to write a letter.
Ask ( ) if she's going to read the newspaper.

Note: Remember: when *who* is the subject, there is no inversion.

Who is going to buy a typewriter?

---

13. **M1**

T: Someone is going to travel to Canada. — S: Who is going to travel to Canada?
Someone is going to take a bus to Canada. — Who is going to take a bus to Canada?
Someone is going to take a train to Canada. — Who is going to take a train to Canada?
Someone is going to drive to Canada. — Who is going to drive to Canada?
Someone is going to take a taxi to Canada. — Who is going to take a taxi to Canada?
Someone is going to run to Canada. — Who is going to run to Canada?

14. **M2**

T: Someone is going to travel to Canada.

S1: Who is going to travel to Canada?
S2: (Ahmed) is.
S3: I'm not going to travel to Canada. I'm going to travel to (New York).

Someone is going to travel to (Mexico).
Someone is going to learn (Spanish).
Someone is going to play (soccer).
Someone is going to take a bus (downtown).
Someone is going to read the (newspaper).
Someone is going to walk to (school).
Someone is going to buy (books).
Someone is going to study (computer science).

15. Negative Answer—Contrast
M2

T: ( ) is going to buy a Rolls-Royce. — S: I'm not going to buy a Rolls-Royce. I'm going to buy a (VW).
( ) is going to travel to Timbuktu. — I'm not going to travel to Timbuktu. I'm going to (visit Paris).

( ) is going to have pizza for breakfast.
( ) is going to walk to (New York).
( ) is going to study Latin.
( ) is going to write a grammar book.
( ) is going to buy a Cadillac.
( ) is going to work at MacDonald's.
( ) is going to take a taxi to Paris.
( ) is going to be in the new movie.

16. **C** T: When are you going to buy a car? S: (Never.) (Next month.)
What are you going to buy next weekend?
Where are you going to buy a new (camera)?
When are you going to travel to (Mexico)?
(Who is going to travel with you?)
(What are you going to do in (Mexico)?
Where are you going to travel this year?
What are you going to do this weekend?
When are you going to see the new movie?
(Who is going to see the movie with you?)
When are you going to study (engineering)?
What are you going to study next year?
Where are you going to study engineering?
Who is going to study (computer science)?
When are you going to cook ( )?
What are you going to cook tomorrow night?
When are you going to eat Saturday night?

17. **C** Ask your classmates. Find out what your neighbor is going to do on the weekend.

Examples:

S1: What are you going to do this weekend? S2: (Look at typewriters.)
Are you going to see the new movie?
Where are you going to travel? When?
Who is going to travel with you?

SECTION TWO

Demonstrative Adjectives and Pronouns

Vocabulary

Nouns	*Adjectives*	*Adverb*
chair	black	over here
model	grammar	
pencil	old	*Phrases*
thing	terrific	a good buy
	reading	a lot (of)
		on sale

Part A. Statements & Questions

At the Department Store

Carlos: What's this?
Salesman: That's our new model. Completely automatic. And the pictures are terrific. We're selling a lot of those.
Chen: Carlos, over here! Look at these typewriters.

Generalization: Demonstratives

Singular	*Plural*
this	these
that	those

this/these = nearer the speaker
that/those = farther from the speaker

---

1. Near and Far Objects
M1 Listen: This book is a grammar book.
That book is a reading book.
This pen is old.
That pen is new.

2. Rep: This book is old.
M1 Sub:

Sub	S:
new	This book is new.
that	That book is new.
pen	That pen is new.
black	That pen is black.
coat	That coat is black.
beautiful	That coat is beautiful.
this	This coat is beautiful.

3. Rep: These chairs are old.
M2 Sub:

Sub	S:
new	These chairs are new.
those	Those chairs are new.
books	Those books are new.
expensive	Those books are expensive.
these	These books are expensive.
pencils	These pencils are expensive.
cheap	These pencils are cheap.
those	Those pencils are cheap.

4.	Rep:	This book is expensive.	S: These books are expensive.
M1		This pen is old.	These pens are old.
		This classroom is nice.	These classrooms are nice.
		This dorm is beautiful.	These dorms are beautiful.
		This camera is cheap.	These cameras are cheap.
		This TV is new.	These TV's are new.

5.	T:	This book is old.	S: These books are old.
M1T		That pen is expensive.	Those pens are expensive.
		This classroom is new.	These classrooms are new.
		That pencil is cheap.	Those pencils are cheap.
		This camera is beautiful.	These cameras are beautiful.
		That typewriter is small.	Those typewriters are small.

6.	T:	typewriter—here—(a good buy)	S: This typewriter is a good buy.
M1T		camera—there	That camera is a good buy.
		TV—there	That TV is a good buy.
		radio—here	This radio is a good buy.
		book—there	That book is a good buy.
		pen—here	This pen is a good buy.
		shirt—here	This shirt is a good buy.
		coat—there	That coat is a good buy.

7. Objects in the classroom

M2	Repeat:	What's this?	It's a pencil.
		What's that?	It's a notebook.
		What are these?	They're pencils.
		What are those?	They're notebooks.

Note: Use this pattern to learn new vocabulary.

---

8. Picture Cue

M2	S1:	What's this?	S2: It's a (car).
		What's this thing?	
		What's that?	
		What are these?	
		What are those?	

Generalization

this/that; these/those are used as pronouns when the object(s) is known to everyone. They are also used in introductions:

"This is my friend, Judy."

9.
C Ask your classmate. Introduce your neighbor to the class. First find out some information about him or her. Then tell the rest of the class.

Example:
S: This is (Laura). She's from Columbia. She's studying English now. She's going to study computer science next year.

Part B. *Wh* Question

Generalization

The question word *which* asks about a choice. It goes in front of a noun or substitutes for it.

Examples:
This book is expensive.

Which book is cheap?
Which is cheap?

---

1. Situation: The store is having a sale. Some things are on sale, some are not.

M1 T: This camera is not on sale. — S: Which camera is on sale?
These radios are not on sale. — Which radios are on sale?
This TV is not on sale. — Which TV is on sale?
These typewriters are not on sale. — Which typewriters are on sale?
This shirt is not on sale. — Which shirt is on sale?
These coats are not on sale. — Which coats are on sale?
This dress is not on sale. — Which dress is on sale?

2. Situation: The store is having a sale. Some things are on sale, some are not.

M2 T: books — S1: (These) books are expensive.
Which books are on sale?
S2: (Those) are.

book — S1: (That) book is expensive.
Which book is on sale?
S2: (This) is.

camera
TV's
radio
typewriters
coats
shirt
dresses
bags
book
pens

3. Picture Cue (Use department store catalogs)
C You are going to have a lot of money. What are you going to buy? Ask your neighbor, too.

Example:
S1: I'm going to buy that camera and this umbrella. Which things are you going to buy?
S2: This ring and that big chair.

4. Picture Cues
C T: These are new cameras.

S1: Which camera (are you going to buy) (are you buying)?
S2: (The large Minolta.)

Here are a lot of houses.
These are new books.
These are restaurants.
Here are a lot of movies.
Here are a lot of new coats.
These are new cars.
Here are a lot of books.
These are TV's.
These are typewriters.
Here are a lot of pens.

SECTION THREE

Possessive Adjectives and Pronouns

Part A. Adjectives

Salesperson: Here's your change. Five dollars and thirty six cents.
Carlos: And my receipt?
Salesperson: Right here. Our warranty is inside, too.
Carlos: OK. Thank you very much.
Salesperson: Thank you. Enjoy your camera.

Vocabulary

Nouns

change
friend
receipt
warranty

Generalization

The possessive forms are the same whether the noun is singular or plural and depend in all cases on the possessor.

Examples:

my camera (my cameras)	our warranty
your change	your radio
his typewriter	their TV
her book	
its color	

1. Rep: The tall boy is my friend.
M1 Sub: her — S: The tall boy is her friend.
his — The tall boy is his friend.
our — The tall boy is our friend.
your — The tall boy is your friend.
their — The tall boy is their friend.
my — The tall boy is my friend.

2. Rep: The boys are my friends.
M1 Sub: our — S: The boys are our friends.
my — The boys are my friends.
your — The boys are your friends.
their — The boys are their friends.
her — The boys are her friends.
his — The boys are his friends.

3. T: Where is Chen's typewriter? — S: His typewriter is here.
M1T Where are the boys' books? — Their books are here.
Where is Carlos' camera? — His camera is here.
Where is Nancy's coat? — Her coat is here.
Where is the teacher's pen? — (Her) pen is here.
Where is your bag? — My bag is here.
Where are ( ) and ( )'s books? — Their books are here.
Where is our classroom? — Our classroom is here.
Where is my bag? — Your bag is here.

4. T: Is this your book? — S: (No, it's his book.)
M2 Is this your coat? — (Yes, it's my coat.)
Are these your pens? — (No, they're her pens.)
Is this your bag?
Is this your classroom?
Is this your chair?
Are these your books?

Are these your pencils?
Is he your friend?
Is she your teacher?

5. What is your country?
C T: (Saudi Arabia) S: That's my country.
(Mexico) That's (her) country.
(Japan) That's (their) country.
(USA) That's (your) country.
(Colombia)
(Switzerland)
(Egypt)
(Venezuela)
(Thailand)
(France)

Part B. Possessive Pronouns

Salesman: Excuse me, is this yours?
Carlos: What is it?
Salesman: An ID, I think.
Carlos: No, its not mine. Oh, it's his . . . my friend's.
Chen! Here's your ID!

Generalization

These pronouns show possession. Note that most are different from the adjectives.

Examples:

my book	— *mine*	our book	— *ours*
your book	— *yours*	your book	— *yours*
his book	— *his*	their book	— *theirs*
her book	— *hers*		

---

1. Rep: That new camera is mine.
M1 That new camera is his.
That new camera is hers.
That new camera is ours.
That new camera is yours.
That new camera is theirs.

2. T: The books are mine. S: They're mine.
M1 The pens are his. They're his.
The notebooks are ours. They're ours.

The pencils are yours. They're yours.
The typewriters are theirs. They're theirs.

3. T: This old Minolta is my camera. S: It's mine.
M1T This old Minolta is her camera. It's hers.
This old Minolta is our camera. It's ours.
This old Minolta is their camera. It's theirs.
This old Minolta is your camera. It's yours.
This old Minolta is his camera. It's his.
This old Minolta is my camera. It's mine.

4. T: This new book is (Laura's). S: It's hers.
M1T That old book is ( )'s. It's his.
This new pen is (teacher's name). It's (hers) (his).
That old pencil is ( )'s. It's his.
This new notebook is ( ) and ( )'s. It's theirs.
That old book is ( ) and yours. It's ours.

Part C. *Whose?*

Chen: Whose is that?
Carlos: It's yours!

Generalization

Someone's typewriter is expensive.
Whose typewriter is expensive? Answer: Chen's.

Whose is the question word indicating possession.

If the subject is known to everyone, *whose* can be a pronoun. *Whose* is the same with singular and plural nouns.

Example: This is my camera. Whose is that?
These are my pennies. Whose are those?

---

1. Rep: Whose pen is that?
M1 Sub: book S: Whose book is that?
pencil Whose pencil is that?
notebook Whose notebook is that?
typewriter Whose typewriter is that?

Rep: Whose pens are these?
Sub: books S: Whose books are these?

pencils	Whose pencils are these?
notebooks	Whose notebooks are these?
typewriters	Whose typewriters are these?

2. Objects in the Classroom (Teacher holds up the items or indicates them.)
M2

T:	bag	S1: Whose bag is this?
		S2: It's (hers).
	chairs	S1: Whose chairs are these?
		S2: They're ours.
	coat	
	pen	
	books	
	pencil	
	bags	
	room	
	coats	

3.
M2

T:	change	S1: Whose change is that?
		S2: It's (mine).
	coats	S1: Whose coats are those?
		S2: They're (ours).
	book	
	pen	
	pencils	
	newspaper	
	chairs	
	notebook	
	classroom	
	books	
	coat	

4. The teacher writes the name of a country on the blackboard.
C Whose country is it?

Example:

T:	Colombia	S1: Whose country is that?
		S2: It's (her) country.
T:	Kuwait	S1: Whose country is that?
		S2: It's (his) country.

Part D. *Who's/Whose*

Note: The pronunciation of *who's* (Pronoun + Be) and *whose* (Possessive) is the same. *Who's* will be followed by an *-ing* form of the verb or an adjective or a noun phrase (Who's going?) (Who's a lawyer?). The possessive *whose* will be followed by a noun (Whose book?) or BE (Whose is this?).

Examples:

A. Someone's going.
Who's going? John.

Someone's late.
Who's late? John.

Someone's from Libya.
Who's from Libya? Ali.

B: Someone's book.
Whose book? John's.

---

1. A = *Who's*
M1T B = *Whose*

T:		S:
	Who's late?	(A)
	Whose book?	(B)
	Whose papers?	(B)
	Who's going?	(A)
	Whose letter?	(B)
	Who's an engineer?	(A)
	Whose camera is that?	(B)
	Whose camera is expensive?	(B)
	Who's the teacher?	(A)
	Whose friend is from the Middle East?	(B)
	Who's the boy from Asia?	(A)

2. T: Who's late? S: (John.)
M2 Whose books? (Mine.)
Who's going to study engineering?
Whose friend is going to study chemistry?
Who's never late?
Who's tall?
Who's from the Middle East?
Whose book?
Whose notebook is that?
Who's going to lunch?

3. Ask your classmates. Find out whose country is in (the Middle East) and find out who
C is going to travel to (the Middle East) this year.

Example:

T: The Middle East

S1: Whose country is in the Middle East?
S2: (Ahmed's)
S1: Who's going to travel to the Middle East this year?
S2: Maybe ( ) and ( ) are.

The Far East
South America

Africa
Europe
Latin America
etc.

SUMMARY DIALOGUE

At the Department Store

1. Carlos: Are you going to look at typewriters today?

2. Chen: Oh, maybe. But I'm not going to buy anything. Are you?

3. Carlos: Yes. A new camera.

4. Chen: These are nice.

5. Salesperson: Those are very nice. All 35 mm. How about this? A real beauty. Just $200 and it's yours.

6. Chen: What's that over there?

7. Salesperson: (Walks over to camera.) This is our automatic model.

8. Chen: How much is it?

9. Salesperson: For this week only our special price is $189.95 plus tax.

10. Chen: That's not so bad.

11. Carlos: Who's buying this camera, you or me?

12. Chen: Not me. I'm just going to take a look at it.

Moments later

13. Salesperson: Here's your change, one dollar and forty-five cents.

14. Carlos: And my receipt?

15. Salesperson: That's inside. With the warranty. Our warranty is good for one year.

16. Carlos: OK. Thank you very much.

17. Salesperson: Thank you. Enjoy your camera. (Carlos moves away.)

18. Salesperson: Excuse me. Is this yours?

19. Chen: What is it?

20. Salesperson: Your ID, I think.

21. Chen: No, its not mine. Oh, it's his . . . my friend's. Carlos, here's your ID.

22. Carlos: (coming over) What?

23. Chen: Your ID!

24. Carlos: Whose?

25. Chen: Yours!

COMMUNICATIVE ACTIVITIES

1) Using the bus is a convenient and (sometimes) cheap way to travel. Find out about routes and fares and report to the class. Note to teachers: Divide up the task among the students and teach them such vocabulary as "Pay-enter," "Exact change," etc. as pertains to your area.

2) Using the money in a foreign country is sometimes confusing, because people have different ways of stating the amount. For example: \$4.95 = four dollars and ninety-five cents, but people usually say "four ninety-five." Also "four ninety-five" could mean \$495.00 if you are talking about expensive cameras or furniture. Listen as your teacher dictates prices as a clerk in a store might say them. Copy down what you hear in numbers. Note to teachers: Check current grocery prices and prices of things the students need to buy, so they can practice with real numbers.

Lesson Four

Bill Jackson's Family

Introduction

Bill Jackson lives with his family in a suburb. Bill commutes to school every day; he takes a street car and a bus, and he arrives at the university at nine o'clock. He stays at the university until five o'clock and then he goes home again. Bill works at a gas station on weekends. He likes science, sports, parties and girls. He doesn't like English. He studies hard, but he doesn't get good grades in English.

Bill has a younger sister. Her name is Jane. She's a sophomore in high school. Jane is going to study at the university in three years.

Mrs. Jackson teaches in the elementary school near their home, and Mr. Jackson works in an office downtown. They have a car, but Mr. Jackson doesn't drive downtown. The traffic is terrible, and parking is very expensive.

Vocabulary

Nouns

- camera
- cheese
- elementary school
- family
- gas station
- grade
- high school
- job
- Mr.
- Mrs.
- office
- parking
- party
- radio
- science
- sister
- sophomore
- sport
- street car
- suburb
- traffic
- typewriter
- weekend
- wine

Adjectives

- elementary
- terrible

Verbs

- advise
- arrive
- build
- commute
- drive
- freeze
- get
- have
- like
- live
- publish
- record
- ride
- stay
- teach
- toast
- wash
- work
- write

Adverbs

- again
- hard
- then
- very

Prepositions

- at
- in
- near
- on
- until
- with

Conjunctions

- and
- or

Phrase

- o'clock

SECTION ONE

Simple Present Tense

Part A. Third Person Singular
Part A-1. Affirmative

Generalization

Previous Patterns

	Subject	*Verb*	*Completer*
Lesson One:	Bill	is	a student,
Lesson Two:	Bill	is studying	engineering.
Lesson Three:	Jane	is going to	study at the university.

New Pattern

Lesson Four:	Bill	studies	hard.

The Simple Present Tense: In spelling, most verbs add *-s* or *-es* to the simple verb for the third person.
Note that *have* is irregular: Bill has a job.

The simple present tense is used for facts and actions which are habitual. It differs from the present continuous (Lesson Two), which denotes actions which are happening now.

---

1. Rep: Bill Jackson lives with his family.
M1 Sub: studies engineering — S: Bill Jackson studies engineering.
lives in a suburb — Bill Jackson lives in a suburb.
has a sister — Bill Jackson has a sister.
arrives at school at 9:00 everyday — Bill Jackson arrives at school at 9:00 everyday.
stays at school until 5:00 — Bill Jackson stays at school until 5:00.
drives the family car — Bill Jackson drives the family car.

2. Rep: Jane likes English class.
M1 Sub: writes letters — S: Jane writes letters.
walks to the park — Jane walks to the park.
takes the bus to school — Jane takes the bus to school.
commutes to school — Jane commutes to school.
works on weekends — Jane works on weekends.
likes English — Jane likes English.

3.	Rep:	Mrs. Jackson teaches science.		
M1	Sub:	watches TV	S:	Mrs. Jackson watches TV.
		teaches in an elementary school		Mrs. Jackson teaches in an elementary school.
		watches TV on weekends		Mrs. Jackson watches TV on weekends.
		teaches a large class		Mrs. Jackson teaches a large class.
		watches the news at 7:00		Mrs. Jackson watches the news at 7:00.
4.	Rep:	Bill lives with his family.		
M1	Sub:	Jane	S:	Jane lives with her family.
		the girl		The girl lives with her family.
		Mrs. Jackson		Mrs. Jackson lives with her family.
		Mr. Jackson		Mr. Jackson lives with his family.
		the woman		The woman lives with her family.
		the man		The man lives with his family.
		Jane		Jane lives with her family.
5.	Rep:	Bill has a typewriter.		
M1	Sub:	a job	S:	Bill has a job.
		a car		Bill has a car.
		a TV		Bill has a TV.
		a radio		Bill has a radio.
		a camera		Bill has a camera.
		a typewriter		Bill has a typewriter.
6.	Rep:	Nancy commutes every day.		
M1T	Sub:	take the bus	S:	Nancy takes the bus every day.
		arrive at 9:00		Nancy arrives at 9:00 every day.
		go to class		Nancy goes to class every day.
		study hard		Nancy studies hard every day.
		have lunch in the cafeteria		Nancy has lunch in the cafeteria every day.
		work at school		Nancy works at school every day.
		take the bus home		Nancy takes the bus home every day.
		watch TV at home		Nancy watches TV at home every day.

Part A-2. Interrogative

Generalization

	Question Formation	*Answer*
Lesson One:	The campus is confusing.	
	Is the campus confusing?	Yes it is.
Lesson Two:	Chen is walking to class.	
	Is Chen walking to class?	Yes he is.

Generalization continues on next page.

Lesson Three: The boys are going to study.
Are the boys going to study? No they aren't.

In these patterns, make questions by placing a form of the verb BE in front of the subject.

New Pattern

Lesson Four: Bill works at a gas station.
Does Bill work at a gas station? Yes he does.

Sentences with simple present tense verbs (third person singular) form questions by placing *does* in front of the subject. Notice what happens to the verb *work*.

Ali: Does Bill take the bus to school every day?
Nancy: Yes, I think he does.
Ali: Why does he live so far from the university?
Nancy: He lives with his parents.

7. Questions about the Jacksons (see p. 00).

M1

T:	S:
Does Bill take the bus to school?	Yes.
Does Bill work at a cafeteria?	No.
Does Bill study English?	Yes.
Does Bill have a sister?	Yes.
Does his sister study at the university?	No.
Does Mr. Jackson teach school?	No.
Does Mr. Jackson work downtown?	Yes.
Does Mrs. Jackson work downtown?	No.
Does Bill live in the dorms?	No.

8.
M1

T:	S:
Bill takes the streetcar.	Does Bill take the streetcar?
Mr. Jackson drives to work.	Does Mr. Jackson drive to work?
The boy works at a gas station.	Does the boy work at a gas station?
The man works downtown.	Does the man work downtown?
Jane goes to high school.	Does Jane go to high school?
Mrs. Jackson teaches in an elementary school.	Does Mrs. Jackson teach in an elementary school?
The girl watches TV every day.	Does the girl watch TV every day?
The woman walks to school.	Does the woman walk to school?
Ali lives near the university.	Does Ali live near the university?
Nancy goes to school at eight o'clock every day.	Does Nancy go to school at eight o'clock every day?

9.	Rep:	Does Bill work in an office?		
M1	Sub:	Jane	S:	Does Jane work at an office?
		drive downtown		Does Jane drive downtown?
		arrive at school at 9:00		Does Jane arrive at school at 9:00?
		the boy		Does the boy arrive at school at 9:00?
		Nancy		Does Nancy arrive at school at 9:00?
		like sports		Does Nancy like sports?
		work at a gas station		Does Nancy work at a gas station?
		Bill		Does Bill work at a gas station?
		the boy		Does the boy work at a gas station?
		have a car		Does the boy have a car?
		have a younger sister		Does the boy have a younger sister?
		the girl		Does the girl have a younger sister?
		Chen		Does Chen have a younger sister?

10.	T:	Does Jane go to school or to work every day?	S:	She goes to school every day.
M1		Does Mr. Jackson work at home or in an office?		He works in an office.
		Does Bill arrive at 9:00 or at 10:00 every day?		He arrives at 9:00 every day.
		Does Mrs. Jackson teach at a high school or at an elementary school?		She teaches at an elementary school.
		Does Bill live downtown or in a suburb?		He lives in a suburb.
		Does Mr. Jackson commute to work or to school?		He commutes to work.
		Does Bill work on weekends or every day?		He works on weekends.
		Does Bill like English or science?		He likes science.
		Does Jane go to high school or to the university?		She goes to high school.

11.	Rep:	Does Bill have a job?		Yes, he does.
M1		Does Jane have a job?		No, she doesn't.
		Does Bill have a younger sister?		Yes, he does.
		Does Jane work downtown?		No, she doesn't.
		Does Mr. Jackson drive to work?		No, he doesn't.
		Does Mrs. Jackson teach in an elementary school?		Yes, she does.

12.	T:	Does Jane work in an office?	S:	No, she doesn't.
M1		Does Bill work on weekends?		Yes, he does.
		Does Mr. Jackson teach school?		No, he doesn't.
		Does Mrs. Jackson work downtown?		No, she doesn't.
		Does Jane go to the university?		No, she doesn't.
		Does Bill arrive at school at 9:00?		Yes, he does.
		Does Jane have an older brother?		Yes, she does.
		Does Bill like English?		No, he doesn't.
		Does Mrs. Jackson teach in an elementary school?		Yes, she does.

13. Rep: Bill takes the bus to school every day.
M1T Sub: tomorrow — S: Bill is going to take the bus to school tomorrow.
every morning — Bill takes the bus to school every morning.
next week — Bill is going to take the bus to school next week.
every Monday — Bill takes the bus to school every Monday.
next Friday — Bill is going to take the bus to school next Friday.
on weekends — Bill takes the bus to school on weekends.
next month — Bill is going to take the bus to school next month.
on weekdays — Bill takes the bus to school on weekdays.

14. T: Jane is a high school student.
M1T
G1: Is Jane a high school student?
G2: Yes, she is.

Bill works in a gas station.
G1: Does Bill work in a gas station?
G2: Yes, he does.

The boys are walking to school.
G1: Are the boys walking to school?
G2: Yes, they are.

Jane goes to high school.
G1: Does Jane go to high school?
G2: Yes, she does.

The high school is good.
G1: Is the high school good?
G2: Yes, it is.

Jane takes the bus.
G1: Does Jane take the bus?
G2: Yes, she does.

Jane is going to study computer science.
G1: Is Jane going to study computer science?
G2: Yes, she is.

Bill studies engineering.
G1: Does Bill study engineering?
G2: Yes, he does.

Bill is going to work next week.
G1: Is Bill going to work next week?
G2: Yes, he is.

15. T: Does ( ) walk to school?
M2
Is ( ) going to the park this afternoon?

Does ( ) speak Arabic?
Is ( ) going to study engineering?
Is ( ) a teacher?
Does ( ) commute to school?
Is ( ) going to buy a camera?
Is ( ) living with a family?
Does ( ) like sports?
Is ( ) an engineer?
Is ( ) going to take the bus downtown tomorrow?
Does ( ) have a younger sister?

S: (Yes, she does.)
(No, she doesn't.)
(Yes, she is.)
(No, she isn't.)

16. T: Ask ( ) if ( ) commutes to school. S1: Does ( ) commute to school?
M2 S2: (Yes, she does.)
(No, she doesn't. She lives in the dorms.)

Ask ( ) if ( ) is going to study biology? S1: Is ( ) going to study biology?
S2: (Yes, he is.)
(No, he isn't. He's going to study chemistry.)

Ask ( ) if ( ) is going downtown this afternoon. S1: Is ( ) going downtown this afternoon?
S2: (Yes, she is.)
(No, he isn't. He's going to the language lab.)

Ask ( ) if ( ) takes the bus to school.
Ask ( ) if ( ) is going to work next year.
Ask ( ) if ( ) is living with a family.
Ask ( ) if ( ) likes TV.
Ask ( ) if ( ) is going downtown today.
Ask ( ) if ( ) has a typewriter.
Ask ( ) if ( ) is having coffee in the cafeteria this afternoon.
Ask ( ) if ( ) arrives at school at nine o'clock.
Ask ( ) if ( ) watches TV in the evening.

17. Find out about your neighbor's family. Ask your classmates.
C
Example Questions:
a) Where does your (mother/father) work?
b) When does he/she arrive at work?
c) Does he take the bus?
d) Does he drive a car?

Part A-3. Negative

Nancy: Bill doesn't drive to school.
Ali: Why not?
Nancy: He doesn't like the heavy traffic.

Generalization

Lesson Two:

Affirmative	Bill *is*	driving to school today.
Negative	Bill *isn't*	driving to school today.

Lesson Four:

Affirmative	Bill	drives to school every day.
Negative	Bill *doesn't*	drive to school every day.

The third singular uses *does* and *not* to form negatives. Usually it is spoken as *doesn't*.

---

1. Rep: Bill doesn't drive to work.
M1 He doesn't have a car.
The woman doesn't take the bus every day.
She doesn't live far from school.
The bus doesn't stop here.
It doesn't go on this street.

2. Rep: Nancy doesn't walk to work every day.
M1 Sub: go — S: Nancy doesn't go to work every day.
take the bus — Nancy doesn't take the bus to work every day.
drive — Nancy doesn't drive to work every day.
walk — Nancy doesn't walk to work every day.
commute — Nancy doesn't commute to work every day.
take the streetcar — Nancy doesn't take the streetcar to work every day.

3. Rep: The woman doesn't like television.
M1 Sub: man — S: The man doesn't like television.
watch — The man doesn't watch television.
movies — The man doesn't watch movies.
student — The student doesn't watch movies.
like — The student doesn't like movies.
the bus — The student doesn't like the bus.
the woman — The woman doesn't like the bus.
take — The woman doesn't take the bus.
street car — The woman doesn't take the street car.

4. T: Bill drives a car. — S: Bill doesn't drive a car.
M1T Chen lives with a family. — Chen doesn't live with a family.
Carlos has a new car. — Carlos doesn't have a new car.
Nancy walks to work. — Nancy doesn't walk to work.
Ali speaks Spanish. — Ali doesn't speak Spanish.
Mr. Jackson drives downtown. — Mr. Jackson doesn't drive downtown.
Mrs. Jackson teaches high school. — Mrs. Jackson doesn't teach high school.
Bill works at home. — Bill doesn't work at home.
Chen commutes to the university. — Chen doesn't commute to the university.

5. T: Ask about ( ) and school. — S1: (Does ( ) take the bus to school?)
C S2: (Yes, she does.)
(No, she doesn't. She walks to school.)

Ask about ( ) and a family. — S1: (Does ( ) live with a family?)
S2: (Yes, he does.)
(No, he doesn't. He lives in the dorms.)

Ask about ( ) and the dorm.
Ask about ( ) and a gas station.
Ask about ( ) and a car.

Ask about ( ) and downtown.
Ask about ( ) and a bus.
Ask about ( ) and a streetcar.
Ask about ( ) and the university.
Ask about ( ) and the park.
Ask about ( ) and the cafeteria.
Ask about ( ) and the language lab.
Ask about ( ) and engineering.
Ask about ( ) and computer science.
Ask about ( ) and a job.

6. T: Ask about ( ) and English *everyday*. S1: (Does ( ) study English every day?)
C S2: (Yes, she does.)
Ask about ( ) and English *today*. S1: (Is ( ) studying English today?)
S2: (No, he isn't. He's going to the park.)
Ask about ( ) and school *everyday/today*.
Ask about ( ) and (biology) *everyday/today*.
Ask about ( ) and the cafeteria *everyday/today*.
Ask about ( ) and the textbook *everyday/today*.
Ask about ( ) and the bus *everyday/today*.

Part B. Third Person Plural
Part B-1. Affirmative

Nancy: These buses go downtown.
Ali: Does number 68 stop here?

Generalization

Singular: The student lives in the dorm.
Plural: The students live in the dorm.
Note: Be careful of the spelling.

There are two differences. The singular verb has an *-s*, the plural subject has an *-s*.

---

1. Listen: The girl studies English. The girls study English.
M1 The student walks to school. The students walk to school.
The streetcar goes downtown. The streetcars go downtown.

2. Listen to the following sentences. If you hear a singular verb, raise your hand;
M1T if you hear a plural, raise two.

T:	Bill lives with his family.	S:	(1)
	Bill and Jane study hard.		(2)
	The boy studies hard.		(1)
	The women study hard.		(2)
	The men drive the car.		(2)
	Mrs. Jackson wants a new car.		(1)
	The women want good jobs.		(2)
	The men need good jobs, too.		(2)
	The Jacksons commute to work.		(2)
	Mr. Jackson takes the bus.		(1)

3. Rep: The students take the bus home at 5:00.
M1

Sub:	go	S:	The students go home at 5:00.
	walk		The students walk home at 5:00.
	take a taxi		The students take a taxi home at 5:00.
	drive		The students drive home at 5:00.
	take a street car		The students take a street car home at 5:00.
	take the bus		The students take the bus home at 5:00.

4. Rep: The women want a car.
M1

Sub:	have	S:	The women have a car.
	a truck		The women have a truck.
	students		The students have a truck.
	need		The students need a truck.
	a bus		The students need a bus.
	the men		The men need a bus.
	drive		The men drive a bus.
	a street car		The men drive a street car.

5.
M1T

T:	The man drives to work.	S:	The men drive to work.
	The car needs gas.		The cars need gas.
	The women teaches school.		The women teach school.
	The girl studies hard.		The girls study hard.
	The boys likes biology.		The boys like biology.
	The woman works downtown.		The women work downtown.
	The girl goes to high school.		The girls go to high school.

6. Rep: The woman drives to work.
M1T

Sub:	students	S:	The students drive to work.
	take a bus		The students take a bus to work.
	to school		The students take a bus to school.
	boy		The boy takes a bus to school.
	take a taxi		The boy takes a taxi to school.
	to college		The boy takes a taxi to college.
	girls		The girls take a taxi to college.
	take a bus		The girls take a bus to college.
	to town		The girls take a bus to town.

7. Rep: The women drive to work every day.
M1T Sub: now — S: The women are driving to work now.
tomorrow — The women are going to drive to work tomorrow.
boys — The boys are going to drive to work tomorrow.
every day — The boys drive to work every day.
now — The boys are driving to work now.
next week — The boys are going to drive to work next week.
professors — The professors are going to drive to work next week.
now — The professors are driving to work now.
every day — The professors drive to work every day.

Part B-2. Interrogative and Short Answers

Generalization

Singular	The boy studies English.	
	Does the boy study English?	Yes, he does. No he doesn't.
Plural	The boys study English.	
	Do the boys study English?	Yes, they do. No, they don't.

---

8. Rep: Do the buses go this way? — No, they don't.
M1 Do the Jacksons have a car? — Yes, they do.
Do the Jacksons live in the city? — No, they don't.
Do the students like exams? — No, they don't.
Do the students like sports? — Yes, they do.
Do the men want a new car? — Yes, they do.

9. Rep: Do the boys commute to school?
M1 Sub: study English — S: Do the boys study English?
live in the dorm — Do the boys live in the dorm?
arrive at school at 9:00 — Do the boys arrive at school at 9:00?
go home at 5:00 — Do the boys go home at 5:00?
take the bus downtown — Do the boys take the bus downtown?
drive to work — Do the boys drive to work?
have a car — Do the boys have a car?
need a thousand dollars — Do the boys need a thousand dollars?
want an airplane — Do the boys want an airplane?

10. Rep: Does the boy take the bus?
M1T Sub: boys — S: Do the boys take the bus?
want a car — Do the boys want a car?
student — Does the student want a car?
students — Do the students want a car?
go to school — Do the students go to school?
girl — Does the girl go to school?
girls — Do the girls go to school?
have a car — Do the girls have a car?

11. T: Does Bill like science? — S: Yes, he does.
M1T Do the Jacksons work at the university? — No, they don't.
Do Bill and Jane work in the city? — No, they don't.
Does Mrs. Jackson teach? — Yes, she does.
Does Bill commute to school? — Yes, he does.
Do the Jacksons live in the city? — No, they don't.
Do Mr. and Mrs. Jackson have jobs? — Yes, they do.
Do the children have cars? — No, they don't.
Does Jane go to elementary school? — No, she doesn't.
Does Bill work at a gas station? — Yes, he does.

Part B-3. Negative

Nancy: Chen doesn't drive to school.
Ali: Chen and Carlos don't have a car.

Generalization

Singular: The man doesn't drive to work.
Plural: The men don't drive to work.

The plural uses *do* + *not* to form negatives. *Do* + *not* is usually pronounced [dont] and written *don't*. It may also be pronounced and written *do not*.

---

12. Rep: The students don't have cars.
M1 The professors don't drive to school.
Carlos and Chen don't live in the suburbs.
The buses don't stop at the university.
The Jacksons don't work downtown.

13. Rep: The Jacksons don't drink California wines.
M1 Sub: like — S: The Jacksons don't like California wines.
New York — The Jacksons don't like New York wines.

		cheese		The Jacksons don't like New York cheese.
		eat		The Jacksons don't eat New York cheese.
		French		The Jacksons don't eat French cheese.
		like		The Jacksons don't like French cheese.
14.	T:	The Jacksons live in the city.	S:	The Jacksons don't live in the city.
M1T		The students like English.		The students don't like English.
		Bill and Jane go to elementary school.		Bill and Jane don't go to elementary school.
		The Jacksons drive a Rolls-Royce.		The Jacksons don't drive a Rolls-Royce.
		Jane and Chen commute to school.		Jane and Chen don't commute to school.
		The students arrive at noon.		The students don't arrive at noon.
		The Jacksons live near the university.		The Jacksons don't live near the university.
15.	T:	The students teach English.		The students don't teach English.
M1T		Mr. Jackson drives to work.		Mr. Jackson doesn't drive to work.
		Mrs. Jackson works at home.		Mrs. Jackson doesn't work at home.
		Carlos and Chen like math.		Carlos and Chen don't like math.
		Jane has a car.		Jane doesn't have a car.
		Bill rides a bicycle to school.		Bill doesn't ride a bicycle to school.
		The Jacksons have a Rolls-Royce.		The Jacksons don't have a Rolls-Royce.
		Bill gets good grades in English.		Bill doesn't get good grades in English.
16.	T:	( ) and ( ) live in the dorm.	S:	( ) and ( ) don't live in the dorm. They live (with a family).
M2		( ) wants a new car.	S:	( ) doesn't want a new car. He wants (a used car).
		( ) speaks French.		
		( ) commutes to school.		
		( ) and ( ) come from Turkey.		
		( ) studies engineering.		
		( ) likes biology.		
		( ) and ( ) take the bus to school.		
		( ) likes (city).		
		( ) and ( ) work in the cafeteria.		
		( ) lives with a family.		
		( ) and ( ) speak Arabic.		
		( ) has a big car.		
17.	T:	Ask if ( ) lives in the dorm.	S1:	Does ( ) live in the dorm?
C			S2:	(Yes, she does.) (No, she doesn't. She lives with a family.)
		Ask if ( ) and ( ) have a car.	S1:	Do ( ) and ( ) have a car?
			S2:	(Yes, they do.) (No, they don't. They walk to school.)
		Ask if ( ) and ( ) commute to school.		
		Ask if ( ) works at a gas station.		
		Ask if ( ) and ( ) speak Spanish.		
		Ask if ( ) likes movies.		

Exercise continues on next page.

Ask if ( ) likes girls.
Ask if ( ) and ( ) live in the dorm.
Ask if ( ) comes from Venezuela.
Ask if ( ) and ( ) come from Libya.
Ask if ( ) studies computer science.
Ask if ( ) and ( ) have a Rolls-Royce.
Ask if ( ) has an apartment.

Part C. First and Second Person

Ali: Do you commute to school every day?
Nancy: Well, I don't, but my friend does.

Generalization

The Question, Short Answer and Negative forms are the same as Third Person Plural.

Examples:
Question/Short Answer

Do you have an apartment?	Yes, we do.
Do you commute to school?	No, I don't.

Negative
We don't have a Rolls-Royce.
I don't like cold weather.

---

1. Listen: I commute to school every day.
M1 Bill and I commute to school every day.
We commute to school every day.
You commute to school every day.

2. Rep: The boys have a car.
M1 Sub:

Sub	S
the girls	The girls have a car.
they	They have a car.
I	I have a car.
We	We have a car.
You	You have a car.
You and John	You and John have a car.
The girls and he	The girls and he have a car.
You and I	You and I have a car.

3. Rep: I want a new roommate.
M1T Sub:

Sub	S
we	We want a new roommate.
the boy	The boy wants a new roommate.
they	They want a new roommate.

	the girls		The girls want a new roommate.
	the woman		The woman wants a new roommate.
	the student		The student wants a new roommate.
	the students		The students want a new roommate.

4. Rep:	The boys have a car.		
M1T Sub:	the boy	S:	The boy has a car.
	I		I have a car.
	we		We have a car.
	the girl		The girl has a car.
	Mr. Jones		Mr. Jones has a car.
	Mr. and Mrs. Jackson		Mr. and Mrs. Jackson have a car.

5. Rep:	We don't like small cars.		
M1T Sub:	I	S:	I don't like small cars.
	the girl		The girl doesn't like small cars.
	the girls		The girls don't like small cars.
	she		She doesn't like small cars.
	we		We don't like small cars.
	Bill		Bill doesn't like small cars.

6. Rep:	Does Chen have a bicycle?		
M1T Sub:	the boys	S:	Do the boys have a bicycle?
	a car		Do the boys have a car?
	Mary		Does Mary have a car?
	the girls		Do the girls have a car?
	an apartment		Do the girls have an apartment?
	Jane		Does Jane have an apartment?
	you		Do you have an apartment?
	bicycle		Do you have a bicycle?

7. T:	Do the Jackson's live in the city?	S:	No, they don't.
M1T	Are Bill and Jane studying now?		Yes, they are.
	Does Bill like science?		Yes, he does.
	Is Bill studying Arabic now?		No, he isn't.
	Is Jane going to go to the university?		Yes, she is.
	Does she go to the university this year?		No, she doesn't.
	Do Mr. and Mrs. Jackson work?		Yes, they do.
	Are they studying now?		No, they aren't.

8. T:	Does ( ) drive to school or take a bus?	S1:	Do you drive to school or take a bus?
M2		S2:	I (take a bus).
	Do ( ) and ( ) live in an apartment or in the dorm?	S1:	Do you and ( ) live in an apartment or in the dorm?
		S2:	We live (in the dorm).
	Are ( ) and ( ) studying Spanish or English?	S1:	Are you and ( ) studying Spanish or English?
		S2:	We're studying English.
	Does ( ) speak ( ) or ( )?		
	Is ( ) speaking English or ( )?		

Exercise continues on next page.

Does ( ) study science or math?
Is ( ) learning English or ( )?
Do ( ) and ( ) come from ( ) or ( )?
Does ( ) like big cars or small cars?
Do ( ) and ( ) want a Honda or a Rolls-Royce?
Do ( ) and I like big cars or small cars?
Does ( ) have an apartment or a room?
Do ( ) and ( ) live near or far from the university?
Are ( ) and ( ) speaking English or ( )?

9. C T: Ask ( ) if he drives to school. — S1: Do you drive to school? S2: (Yes, I do.) (No, I don't. I take a bus.)

Ask ( ) if she's studying math. — S1: Are you studying math? S2: (Yes, I am.) (No, I'm not. I'm going to study math next year.)

Ask ( ) if he takes the bus.
Ask ( ) if she lives near the university.
Ask ( ) if he is speaking Spanish now.
Ask ( ) if he has lunch in the cafeteria.
Ask ( ) if ( ) is having coffee now.
Ask ( ) if she wants a new car.
Ask ( ) if he is going to New York next weekend.
Ask ( ) if she takes a trip every weekend.
Ask ( ) if he and ( ) have a Rolls-Royce.
Ask ( ) if ( ) and ( ) speak Arabic.
Ask ( ) if ( ) and ( ) are buying a car.

SECTION TWO

Wh Questions

Who? (Subject)

Note: Someone wants a Rolls-Royce.
Who wants a Rolls-Royce?

(Chen) does.
(Chen and Bill) do.

Who has either singular or plural referent, but the verb is always 3rd singular when *who* is its subject.

---

1. T: Someone commutes to work. S: Who commutes to work?
M1
Someone goes to school every day. — Who goes to school every day?
Someone teaches elementary school. — Who teaches elementary school?
Someone works downtown. — Who works downtown?
Someone takes a bus to school. — Who takes a bus to school?
Someone like science. — Who likes science?

2. T: Someone commutes to school. S1: Who commutes to school?
M2 S2: (( ) does.) (( ) and ( ) do.)

Someone wants a Rolls-Royce.
Someone has an apartment.
Someone lives with an American family.
Someone lives in the dorm.
Someone takes the bus to school.
Someone walks to school.
Someone lives near the university.
Someone drives to school.
Someone works on weekends.
Someone teaches school.
Someone works downtown.

What? (Object)

Generalization

Statement:	Bill wants something.	
Yes/No Question:	Does Bill want something?	Answer: Yes, he does.
Wh Question:	What does Bill want?	A Rolls-Royce.

---

3. Rep: What does Bill want?
M1
What do you drive?
What do we need?
What does Ali study?
What do you like?
What does Mrs. Jackson teach?

4. T: Bill needs something. G1: Does Bill need something?
M1T G2: What does Bill need?

Jane wants something. G1: Does Jane want something?
G2: What does Jane want?

Jane and Bill study something. G1: Do Jane and Bill study something?
G2: What do Jane and Bill study?

Chen studies something. G1: Does Chen study something?
G2: What does Chen study?

Exercise continues on next page.

Chen has something.	G1:	Does Chen have something?
	G2:	What does Chen have?
The boys want something.	G1:	Do the boys want something?
	G2:	What do the boys want?
They have something.	G1:	Do they have something?
	G2:	What do they have?
Carlos likes something.	G1:	Does Carlos like something?
	G2:	What does Carlos like?
Chen watches something.	G1:	Does Chen watch something?
	G2:	What does Chen watch?

5. T: Bill needs something. — S: What does he need?
M1T
Chen has something. — What does he have?
Bill and Chen study something. — What do they study?
Nancy likes something. — What does she like?
They want something. — What do they want?
We need something. — What do we need?
She needs something. — What does she need?
You want something. — What do you want?

6. T: Ask ( ) what he wants. — S1: What do you want?
C
S2: I want (a new camera).

Ask ( ) what ( ) wants. — S1: What does ( ) want?
S2: He wants (a new car).

Ask ( ) what ( ) and ( ) need.
Ask ( ) what he drives.*
Ask ( ) what ( ) needs.
Ask ( ) what ( ) and ( ) want.
Ask ( ) what I want.
Ask ( ) what he studies.
Ask ( ) what ( ) teaches.
Ask ( ) what ( ) drives.
Ask ( ) what he smokes.**

Where?

Generalization

Statement:			Bill lives	somewhere.		
Yes/No Question:		Does	Bill live	somewhere?	Answer:	Yes, he does.
Wh Question:	Where	does	Bill live?			In the suburbs.

---

*This refers to the make of car (e.g. VW, Chevrolet).
**This refers to pipe, cigar, or brand of cigarettes.

7. T: Jane lives somewhere now. S: Where does Jane live now?
M1
Jane studies somewhere every day. — Where does Jane study every day?
The students go somewhere every day. — Where do the students go every day?
The girls take the bus somewhere every day. — Where do the girls take the bus everyday?
The girl walks somewhere every day. — Where does the girl walk every day?
The boys go somewhere every Saturday. — Where do the boys go every Saturday?
Chen studies somewhere every night. — Where does Chen study every night?
The boys go somewhere every weekend. — Where do the boys go every weekend?

8. T: Ask ( ) where she lives. S1: Where do you live?
M2 S2: (In the dorm.) (On ( ) street.)

Ask ( ) where ( ) lives.
Ask ( ) where ( ) and ( ) live.
Ask ( ) where ( ) comes from.
Ask ( ) where she comes from.
Ask ( ) where ( ) and ( ) come from.
Ask ( ) where he studies.
Ask ( ) where ( ) studies.
Ask ( ) where she goes every day at 3:00.
Ask ( ) where ( ) goes every day at 10:00.
Ask ( ) where he waits for the bus.
Ask ( ) where ( ) lives.
Ask ( ) where she eats dinner.
Ask ( ) where ( ) goes on weekends.

When?

Generalization

Statement:			Bill goes	to school	sometimes.	
Yes/No Question:		Does	Bill go	to school	sometimes?	Yes, he does.
Wh Question:	When	does	Bill go	to school?		Every day.

---

9. T: Ali drives to school sometimes. S: When does Ali drive to school?
M1
The girl studies sometimes. — When does the girl study?
The men commute to work sometimes. — When do the men commute to work?
Nancy goes to school sometimes. — When does Nancy go to school?
The boys walk to school sometimes. — When do the boys walk to school?
The women go to class sometimes. — When do the women go to class?
The students work sometimes. — When do the students work?
The boy drives to school sometimes. — When does the boy drive to school?

10. T: Ask ( ) when she arrives at school. S1: When do you arrive at school?
M2 S2: (In the morning.)

Exercise continues on next page.

Ask ( ) when he does his homework.
S1: When do you do your homework?
S2: (All the time.)

Ask ( ) when she arrives home every day.
Ask ( ) when she studies.
Ask ( ) when he reads (Arabic) newspapers.
Ask ( ) when she has lunch.
Ask ( ) when he watches TV.
Ask ( ) when she listens to the radio.
Ask ( ) when he goes to work.
Ask ( ) when she arrives at the university.
Ask ( ) when she takes the bus downtown.
Ask ( ) when he writes letters.

11. M2 T: Ask ( ) who studies English.
S1: Who studies English?
S2: (Jose) does.
S3: Does (Luis) study English?
S4: No, he doesn't.
S3: What does he study?
S4: He studies (economics).
S3: Where does he study?
S4: (At the university.)
S3: When does he study?
S4: (Every day.)

Ask ( ) who takes a bus to school.
Ask ( ) who drives a VW.
Ask ( ) who lives with a family.
Ask ( ) who has an apartment.
Ask ( ) who lives in a dorm.
Ask ( ) who likes mathematics.
Ask ( ) who studies engineering.
Ask ( ) who goes to the library every day.
Ask ( ) who works on weekends.
Ask ( ) who gets good grades in English.
Ask ( ) who likes American food.
Ask ( ) who goes to American movies.

12. C T: What are you studying?
S: (I'm studying English.)
Who commutes to school?
Who takes the bus to school?
Where do you study?
Do you study every day? What? When?
What does ( ) study?
Who is going to study ( )?
Where are you going to study next year?
What are you going to study next year?
Where do you have lunch? When?
Do you speak ( ) sometimes? When?

13. T: Find out when ( ) eats dinner.
C

S1: (When do you eat dinner?)
S2: (Around 6:00.)

Find out where ( ) and ( ) have lunch.

S1: (Where do you and ( ) have lunch?)
S2: (At the Student Union cafeteria.) (We go to a different place every day.)

Find out what ( ) does on weekends.
Find out what ( ) is going to do tomorrow after class.
Find out where ( ) and ( ) study.
Find out when ( ) and ( ) watch TV.
Find out where ( ) is going after class.
Find out what ( ) drives.
Find out who is going to visit the class next week.
Find out what ( ) does in his spare time.
Find out who eats lunch at the Student Union.
Find out where ( ) and ( ) live.
Find out when ( ) reads newspapers in his language.
Find out what ( ) reads for pleasure.

14. Ask your classmates. Ask your neighbor questions like the questions you have learned.
C Find out as much information as you can.

Example:

Where do you live? (I live in an apartment, on ( ) street.)
Do you drive a car to school? (No, I walk or take the bus.)
When do you arrive? (Oh, early in the morning.)

Impersonal *You*

Note: Use this pattern when you want to know a spelling. *You* in this question is impersonal and not answered by *I*, but merely by giving the spelling. Other examples of impersonal *you*: "How do you get downtown?" "You take a bus." "Which bus do you take to get downtown?" "No. 75, 76 or 79."

---

15. Rep: How do you spell "suburb"?
M1 Sub: pollution — S: How do you spell "pollution"?
streetcar — How do you spell "streetcar"?
bicycle — How do you spell "bicycle"?
commute — How do you spell "commute"?
weather — How do you spell "weather"?

16. T:	dictionary	S1: How do you spell "dictionary"?
M1T		S2: D-I-C-T-I-O-N-A-R-Y.
	office	S1: How do you spell "office"?
		S2: O-F-F-I-C-E.
	cigar	S1: How do you spell "cigar"?
		S2: C-I-G-A-R.
	movies	S1: How do you spell "movies"?
		S2: M-O-V-I-E-S.
	bicycle	S1: How do you spell "bicycle"?
		S2: B-I-C-Y-C-L-E.
	lecture	S1: How do you spell "lecture"?
		S2: L-E-C-T-U-R-E.
	politics	S1: How do you spell "politics"?
		S2: P-O-L-I-T-I-C-S.
	suburb	S1: How do you spell "suburb"?
		S2: S-U-B-U-R-B.

SECTION THREE

Agent Nouns

Generalization

Many verbs can be changed into agent nouns (*one who/thing which*) by adding *er/or* to the simple form of the verb. The pronunciation of *er* and *-or* is the same.

Verb	*Noun*
teach	teacher
dance	dancer
counsel	counselor

---

1. Listen to the descriptions of the jobs.

M1 T:

T	S
The man teaches English.	He's a teacher.
The woman counsels students.	She's a counselor.
The man advises students.	He's an advisor.
The woman drives a bus.	She's a driver.
The man commutes to the university.	He's a commuter.
The woman sings in the school play.	She's a singer.
The man runs every morning.	He's a runner.
The woman writes textbooks.	She's a writer.

	The man edits our school newspaper.		He's an editor.
	The woman manages the business.		She's a manager.

2. Situation: The Jacksons have a lot of appliances in their home.

M1T T:	To wash the clothes—	S:	To wash the clothes, you need a washer.
	To dry the clothes—		To dry the clothes, you need a dryer.
	To freeze the food—		To freeze the food, you need a freezer.
	To refrigerate food—		To refrigerate food, you need a refrigerator.
	To toast bread—		To toast bread, you need a toaster.
	To sharpen knives—		To sharpen knives, you need a sharpener.
	To mix the ingredients—		To mix the ingredients you need a mixer.
	To heat the room—		To heat the room, you need a heater.

3. T:	He's a teacher.	S1:	Does he teach (English)?
M2		S2:	No, he is a (French) teacher.
	She's a writer.	S1:	Does she write (textbooks)?
		S2:	No, she's a (cookbook) writer.
	He's a translator.		
	He's a collector.		
	She's a publisher.		
	He's a builder.		
	She's a singer.		
	He's an editor.		
	He's an advisor.		
	He's a manager.		
	They're writers.		

4. T:	toast	S1:	I'm (going to the department store to get) a toaster.
C		S2:	Why do you (need) a toaster?
		S1:	To toast (the bread for breakfast).
	wash	S1:	I'm (going to Sears to buy) a washer.
		S2:	Why do you (want) a washer?
		S1:	To wash (the clothes) (the dishes).
	refrigerate		
	light		
	dry		
	record		
	sharpen		
	open		
	freeze		
	heat		
	cool		

SECTION FOUR

Object Pronouns

Ali: Bill studies biology. He likes it.
Nancy: I see him in the lab every day.

Generalization

Most of the subject pronouns have different forms when they are the object of the verb.

Examples:

Subject	*Object*
I	me
we	us
you	you
it	it
he	him
she	her
they	them

---

1. Rep: Ali likes the book. — He likes it.
M1
Ali likes the man. — He likes him.
Ali likes the woman. — He likes her.
Ali likes the students. — He likes them.
Ali likes the boys and me. — He likes you.
Ali likes you and me. — He likes us.
Ali likes (Nancy). — He likes her.

2. T: I can teach biology. — S: I can teach it.
M1T
I can teach the man. — I can teach him.
I can teach the boys. — I can teach them.
I can teach the girl. — I can teach her.
She can teach you and me. — She can teach us.
She can teach Bill and me. — She can teach you.
She can teach Bill and Jane. — She can teach them.

3. T: Do you like (English)? — S: (Yes, I like it.)
M2/C
(No, I don't like it.)
Are you teaching (Bill) (Spanish)? — (Yes, I'm teaching him Spanish.)
(No, I'm teaching him Arabic.)

Do you drive ( ) to school?
Are you going to teach ( ) and ( )
(language)?
Do you like (Americans)?
Is ( ) going to teach ( ) and ( )
(language)?
Does ( ) like (subject)?
(Etc.)

SUMMARY DIALOGUE

Talking About Bill

1. Carlos: Do you know Bill?

2. Nancy: Yeah, I do.

3. Carlos: Does he live in the dorms?

4. Nancy: No, he doesn't. He lives at home.

5. Carlos: Where's that?

6. Nancy: Why are you so interested?

7. Carlos: I'm just curious about people. I like Bill.

8. Nancy: I guess he's OK. I don't know him very well. He lives with his parents in the suburbs. He commutes every day.

9. Carlos: I'm sorry, what does that mean?

10. Nancy: "Commutes"? That means he travels to school every day.

11. Carlos: How do you spell that?

12. Nancy: C-O-M-M-U-T-E-S. Are you writing that down?

13. Carlos: Yes. I try to learn ten new words a day.

14. Nancy: Boy, you're serious.

15. Carlos: Well, not all the time. Do you live on campus?

16. Nancy: No, I share an apartment with a friend.

17. Carlos: Do you commute to school?

18. Nancy: No, I don't have a car, and I don't like the bus. My apartment is not far away. I walk to school every day. Where do <u>you</u> live?

19. Carlos: I'm living in a dorm this term. Next term we're going to find an apartment.

20. Nancy: Who's "we"?

21. Carlos: Chen and I. Do you know him?

22. Nancy: I think so. He's in our chemistry class, right?

23. Carlos: Yeah. We're looking for an apartment already.

24. Nancy: Well, good luck. I'll talk to you later, all right? I'm late for my French class.

25. Carlos: OK, au revoir.

COMMUNICATIVE ACTIVITIES

1) Discussion. When young people from your country go to University, is it common to live away from the family? Do they live in dormitories? Where do they eat? Do they sometimes live in apartments? Is it expensive for the family?

2) Vending Machines. Using vending machines in the U.S. can be a problem if you don't know the names of the coins associated with certain values.

Value	*Name*
.01	penny
.05	nickel
.10	dime
.25	quarter
.50	fifty cents or half dollar

Problem: Find a vending machine which has something you want or like. How much is it? What coins do you need? Will the machine give change? Report to the class.

Note to teachers: Have coins for the students to handle. Set problems of making change for practice with the numbers. Also explain any vagaries of local vending machines, such as existence of a dollar changer, the need for exact change, etc.

Lesson Five

Host(ess) Gifts

Introduction

Chen has been invited to dinner in an American home. He wants to take a gift, but he doesn't know what to buy.

Chen: Bill, give me some advice.

Vocabulary

Nouns

Count			Non-count	
apple	flower	newspaper	advice	macaroni
banana	fruit	painting	bacon	milk
book	gift	party	beer	money
candy	gift shop	peach	bread	music
candle	hamburger	problem	coffee	plan
carrot	hour	rose	electricity	rice
cigarette	idea	sandwich	fish	salt
chicken	invitation	suggestion	food	spaghetti
clerk	magazine	supermarket	help	sugar
coaster	map	tuna	ice cream	tea
coin	meat	vase	lettuce	
custom	minute	vegetable		
dollar	movie	*groceries		
egg	neighbor	*refreshments		

*As nouns, these words are usually in the plural form.

Verbs			*Adjectives*	*Expressions*
arrive	get (obtain)	read	all right	free time
buy	give	smoke	fresh	to go shopping
cook	have	spend	inexpensive	lottery ticket
drink	need	want	nice	(shopping) mall
eat				

SECTION ONE

Count/Non-Count Nouns

Part A. Indefinite Noun Phrase—Affirmative

Generalization

I need some books.
I need some help. (some = a quantity of)

There are two main groups of nouns in English:

1) Count Nouns

They can be counted. They have singular and plural forms:

book/books

2) Non-count Nouns

They are not usually counted. They have only one form:

advice, help

Note: Previous Pattern: I need a book.
New Pattern: I need some books.

---

1. Situation: Chen wants a gift for the Wilsons.
M1 Rep: I need some ideas.

Sub:	S:
suggestions	I need some suggestions.
flowers	I need some flowers.
coasters	I need some coasters.
candles	I need some candles.
paintings	I need some paintings.
ideas	I need some ideas.

2. Situation: Bill is going to the supermarket for groceries.
M1 Rep: I want some milk.

Sub:	S:
bread	I want some bread.
meat	I want some meat.

bacon — I want some bacon.
ice cream — I want some ice cream.
beer — I want some beer.
fruit — I want some fruit.
rice — I want some rice.

3. Rep: I want some apples.
M1 Sub: banana — S: I want some bananas.
vegetable — I want some vegetables.
carrot — I want some carrots.
cigarette — I want some cigarettes.
peach — I want some peaches.
orange — I want some oranges.

4. Situation: Nancy is buying a lot of things.
M1T Rep: I have some bread.
Sub: fruit — S: I have some fruit.
apple — I have some apples.
banana — I have some bananas.
vegetable — I have some vegetables.
ice cream — I have some ice cream.
coffee — I have some coffee.
carrot — I have some carrots.
lettuce — I have some lettuce.
tea — I have some tea.

5. Chain Exercise—Alternate Count and Non-Count Nouns.
M2 T: What are you buying?
S1: I'm buying some (vegetables).
S2: S/he's buying some vegetables and I'm buying some (milk).
S3: S/he's buying some vegetables and s/he's buying some milk and I'm buying some (apples).

6. T: You're going to have a party.
C What do you need?
S1: We need some (music).
S2: We need some (beer) (refreshments).

Part B. Interrogative and Negative

Bill: Do you have any gifts from your country?
Chen: I have some paintings.

Generalization

I need some advice/suggestions.

Do you need {some / any} advice/suggestions?

I don't need any advice/suggestions.

Some is used in affirmative sentences and sometimes in questions.
Any is used in negative sentences and in questions. It means an indefinite quantity.

Some and *any* are used with both count and non-count nouns.

---

1. Ali is going to the supermarket.
M1 Rep: Do you need any sugar?

Sub:		S:
	help	Do you need any help?
	vegetables	Do you need any vegetables?
	cigarettes	Do you need any cigarettes?
	milk	Do you need any milk?
	bread	Do you need any bread?
	oranges	Do you need any oranges?

2. The clerk is talking to Ali.
M1 Rep: No, we don't have any bananas.

Sub:		S:
	fruit	No, we don't have any fruit.
	vegetables	No, we don't have any vegetables.
	coffee	No, we don't have any coffee.
	beer	No, we don't have any beer.
	cigarettes	No, we don't have any cigarettes.
	eggs	No, we don't have any eggs.

3. It's late Saturday afternoon, and you're buying groceries. The store is out of many things. Ask the clerk.
M1T T:

T:	
fresh vegetables	S1: Do you have any fresh vegetables?
carrots and lettuce	S2: We have some carrots and lettuce.
fresh bread/no	S1: Do you have any fresh bread?
	S2: No, we don't have any fresh bread.

fresh fruit/apples and bananas
fresh eggs/no
meat/hamburger and chicken
macaroni/no
fish/tuna
coffee/no

Part C. Expressions of Quantity

Part C-1. *A lot of*

Bill: Does she use a lot of candles?
Chen: No, not a lot.

Generalization

I need some help.
I need a lot of help.
Do you read a lot of magazines?

A lot of = a large quantity. The expression is used with count and non-count nouns.

---

1. Rep: He needs a lot of groceries.
M1 Sub:

	S:
eggs	He needs a lot of eggs.
milk	He needs a lot of milk.
candy	He needs a lot of candy.
meat	He needs a lot of meat.
vegetables	He needs a lot of vegetables.
rice	He needs a lot of rice.

2. **M1T**

T:	S:
Chen needs groceries.	Does he need a lot of groceries?
Ali buys rice.	Does he buy a lot of rice?
Nancy wants coffee.	Does she want a lot of coffee?
Carlos and Bill need cigarettes.	Do they need a lot of cigarettes?
Jane buys vegetables.	Does she buy a lot of vegetables?
Chen want food.	Does he want a lot of food?

Part C-2. *Much/Many*

Chen: I dont't have much money. I can't buy many things.

Generalization

Much and *many* both mean *a lot of.*
Much and *many* are both used in questions and negative statements.

Example:

Question: Do you need {a lot / much} of help?

Generalization continues on next page.

What kind of nouns go with *much*? (Non-count nouns)

What kind of nouns go with *many*? (Count nouns)

---

1. Rep: He doesn't have much money.
M1 Sub: need-help — S: He doesn't need much help.

need-help	He doesn't need much help.
want-advice	He doesn't want much advice.
spend-money	He doesn't spend much money.
buy-food	He doesn't buy much food.
eat-bread	He doesn't eat much bread.
drink-coffee	He doesn't drink much coffee.

2. Rep: We don't buy many groceries.
M1 Sub: S:

eat-vegetables	We don't eat many vegetables.
buy-eggs	We don't buy many eggs.
want-cigarettes	We don't want many cigarettes.
need-suggestions	We don't need many suggestions.
read-newspapers	We don't read many newspapers.
buy-book	We don't buy many books.
have-ideas	We don't have many ideas.

3. **M1** T: S:

Do you drink much milk?	No, I don't drink much milk.
Do you read many newspapers?	No, I don't read many newspapers.
Do you have much money?	No, I don't have much money.
Do you smoke many cigarettes?	No, I don't smoke many cigarettes.
Do you drink much beer?	No, I don't drink much beer.
Do you have many books?	No, I don't have many books.
Do you have much homework?	No, I don't have much homework.

4. **M1T** T: S:

Do you eat a lot of rice?	No, I don't eat much rice.
Do you read a lot of books?	No, I don't read many books.
Do you drink a lot of milk?	No, I don't drink much milk.
Do you spend a lot of money?	No, I don't spend much money.
Do you give a lot of advice?	No, I don't give much advice.
Do you have a lot of ideas?	No, I don't have many ideas.
Do you see a lot of movies?	No, I don't see many movies.
Do you buy a lot of bread?	No, I don't buy much bread.
Do you buy a lot of cigarettes?	No, I don't buy many cigarettes.
Do you need a lot of help?	No, I don't need much help.

5. **C** Suppose you arrive in a new city/country. What do you need? What are you going to buy?
S1: I need a lot of (money). I don't need much (advice).
S2: I want (some maps).

6. **C** You are going to get $1,000,000 from a lottery ticket. Tell the class what you're going to do with it. Tell what you're <u>not</u> going to do.
S: (I'm going to buy a lot of new cars. I'm not going to do much work.)

Part E. *A little/a few*

Chen: Give me a little help.
Bill: Chen, I only have a few minutes.

Generalization

A little is the opposite of *much*.
A few is the opposite of *many*.

A little and *a few* are used mainly in affirmative statements:

I need a few dollars. I have a little money.

Which expression is used with count nouns? (*A few*)

Which expression is used with non-count nouns? (*A little*)

Count: a lot of/many/a few
Non-Count: a lot of/much/a little

---

1. Eating Habits

		T:	S:
M1	T:	I eat a lot of rice.	I eat a little rice.
		I drink a lot of beer.	I drink a little beer.
		I buy a lot of bread.	I buy a little bread.
		I cook a lot of spaghetti.	I cook a little spaghetti.
		I need a lot of food.	I need a little food.
		I use a lot of salt.	I use a little salt.

2. T: I read a lot of books. S: I read a few books.

T:	S:
I read a lot of books.	I read a few books.
I read a lot of newspapers.	I read a few newspapers.
I see a lot of movies.	I see a few movies.
I buy a lot of gifts.	I buy a few gifts.
I need a lot of cigarettes.	I need a few cigarettes.
I have a lot of suggestions.	I have a few suggestions.

3. Time/Money/Food

M1T

T:	S:
time	I have a little time.
minutes	I have a few minutes.
hours	I have a few hours.
days	I have a few days.
money	I have a little money.
dollars	I have a few dollars.
coins	I have a few coins.
food	I have a little food.
sandwiches	I have a few sandwiches.

4. Imagine that your classmates are going to (the mall).

M2 T: ( ) wants a little ( ).
( ) buys a few ( ).
( ) doesn't smoke many ( ).
( ) has a few ( ).
( ) spends a little ( ).
( ) doesn't buy many ( ).
( ) doesn't have much ( ).
( ) eats a little ( ).
( ) drinks a little ( ).
( ) cooks a few ( ).

S: (Ali) wants a little (advice).
(Nancy) buys a few (books).

Part F. *Wh* Questions

Chen: How many things are nice and inexpensive?
Bill: Not many. How much money are you going to spend?
Chen: About ten dollars.

Generalization

The *Wh* questions for all the expressions of quantity are:

how much
how many

Which one is used for count nouns? (How many?)
Which one is used for non-count nouns? (How much?)

---

1. Nancy is going shopping.

M1 Rep: How much food do you need?

Sub:	S:
bread	How much bread do you need?
fruit	How much fruit do you need?
bacon	How much bacon do you need?
macaroni	How much macaroni do you need?
rice	How much rice do you need?
beer	How much beer do you need?
coffee	How much coffee do you need?

2. Ali is going out to dinner tonight. Now he's shopping for a gift.

M1	Rep: How many gifts do you want?		
	Sub: flowers	S:	How many flowers do you want?
	roses		How many roses do you want?
	coasters		How many coasters do you want?
	vases		How many vases do you want?
	candles		How many candles do you want?
	paintings		How many paintings do you want?

3. ( ) is going grocery shopping.

M1T	T: eggs	S:	How many eggs does (she) need?
	milk		How much milk does she need?
	bread		How much bread does she need?
	apples		How many apples does she need?
	bananas		How many bananas does she need?
	rice		How much rice does she need?

4.	T: money/for school	S1:	How much money do you need for school?
M2		S2:	(About two thousand dollars.)
	books/for school	S1:	How many books do you need for school?
		S2:	(Maybe ten or twelve.)
	money/for food		
	books/for class		
	flowers/for gifts		
	money/for books		
	eggs/for breakfast		
	meat/for dinner		
	beer/for the party		
	vegetables/for dinner		
	coffee/for breakfast		

5.	T: free time—have	S1:	How much free time do you have (every day)?
C		S2:	(I don't have any free time.) (I don't have much free time.) (A few hours.)
	cigarettes—smoke	S1:	How many cigarettes do you smoke (every week).
		S2:	(I smoke a lot of (a few) cigarettes.) (I don't smoke.)
	rice—eat		
	bread—buy		
	beer—drink		
	candy—eat		
	money—spend		
	books—read		
	gifts—buy		
	letters—write		
	newspapers—read		

6. Ask your classmates. Find out how your neighbor plans a party in his or her
C country.

Example 1: S1: How much food do you need?
S2: (A lot. In my country people eat a lot at parties.)

Example 2: S1: How many people do you invite.
S2: (Not many. Parties in my country are small.)

SECTION TWO

Request/Suggestion Forms

Vocabulary

Nouns	*Verbs*		*Adjectives*	*Expressions*
brother	begin	practice	angry	a while
cafeteria	bring	sign	fast	be on time
door	call	sit	hard	go downtown
exercise	close	speak	late	go for a walk
homework	come	stop	prompt	
lunch	drive	study	slow	*Adverbs*
taxi	finish	visit	younger	clearly
window	leave	wait		now
	lose	walk		
	open	write		
	play			

Part A. Request

Chen: Bill, please give me some advice.

Generalization

The request forms are the same as the present tense of the verb, except for BE.

Examples: Please be on time.
Please don't be angry.

1. Rep: Please give me some advice.
M1
Please speak English.
Please come to class on time.
Please be on time.
Please do the homework.
Please be prompt.
Please open the window.
Please close the door.
Please write clearly.

2.	T:	Ask ( ) to speak English in class.	S1:	Please speak English in class.
M1T		( ) answer OK	S2:	OK
		Ask ( ) to be on time to class.	S:	Please be on time to class.
		Ask ( ) to close the door.		Please close the door.
		Ask ( ) to finish her homework.		Please finish your homework.
		Ask ( ) to speak slowly.		Please speak slowly.
		Ask ( ) to sign his name.		Please sign your name.
		Ask ( ) to wait a minute.		Please wait a minute.
		Ask ( ) to come at 5:00.		Please come at 5:00.
		Ask ( ) to bring his car.		Please bring your car.
		Ask ( ) to drive slowly.		Please drive slowly.

3. Rep: Please don't be late.
M1
Please don't speak Spanish.
Please don't lose your books.
Please don't open the window.
Please don't do your homework in class.

4.	T:	Ask ( ) not to speak (native language) in class.	S1:	Please don't speak (Arabic) in class.
M1T			S2:	OK
		Ask ( ) not to be late.	S:	Please don't be late.
		Ask ( ) not to speak so fast.		Please don't speak so fast.
		Ask ( ) not to do his homework in class.		Please don't do your homework in class.
		Ask ( ) not to spend so much money.		Please don't spend so much money.
		Ask ( ) not to drink so much beer.		Please don't drink so much beer.
		Ask ( ) not to drive so fast.		Please don't drive so fast.
		Ask ( ) not to be angry.		Please don't be angry.

5. Make a Request of Your Friend

M2	T:	Ask your friend to do something.	S:	(Please open the window.)
		Ask your friend not to do something.		(Please don't smoke in the classroom.)

6. Your younger brother is going to school in the USA. Give him some advice.
C
Examples: Study hard.
Don't lose your money.

Part B. Suggestion (self included)

Chen: Bill, let's go to the gift shop.

Generalization

This pattern is used for suggestions. You agree by saying: "OK," "Sure" or "Great." You disagree by saying "Let's not" and then making another suggestion.

Remember: It's not polite to say "Let's not" without making another suggestion.

---

1. Rep: Let's go to the gift shop.
M1 Let's go downtown.
Let's have a party.
Let's get a cup of coffee.
Let's do the homework.
Let's have lunch at the cafeteria.

2. T: Make a suggestion.
M2 The next student disagrees. (Make sure the alternate suggestions are realistic.)

Examples: S1: Let's (go downtown).
S2: Let's not go downtown.
Let's go (to a movie).
S3: Let's not go to a movie. Let's (get a cup of coffee).

Part C. *Shall*

Bill: Shall we go now?
Chen: Yes, let's.

Generalization

The suggestion form with *shall* is like *let's* and can be used in formal and informal situations. It has the question (rising) intonation and is the only common use of the word *shall* in American English.

---

1. Rep: Shall we go?
M1 Sub: begin — S: Shall we begin?
stop — Shall we stop?
do the exercises — Shall we do the exercises?
go now — Shall we go now?

2. T: Let's go. — S: Shall we go?
M1 Let's stop. — Shall we stop?
Let's leave. — Shall we leave?
Let's get some coffee. — Shall we get some coffee?
Let's buy some ice cream. — Shall we buy some ice cream?
Let's cook spaghetti tonight. — Shall we cook spaghetti tonight?

Note: Short answers for the *shall* pattern.

Example:
Shall we go? Yes, let's.
No, let's not. (Let's stay here a while).

---

3. T: go now — S1: Shall we go now?
M2
S2: Yes, let's.
S3: No, let's not. (Let's stay here a while).

buy some ice cream — S1: Shall we buy some ice cream?
S2: Yes, let's.
S3: No, let's not. (Let's buy some candy).

stop at the supermarket
get some eggs
buy spaghetti
cook rice tonight
have lunch at McDonald's
take a taxi to the Wilsons' house
buy candles as a gift

4. T: Make a suggestion. Use *shall.*
C
S2: agrees or disagrees

Example: S1: Shall we (go the Student Union for a cup of coffee)?
S2: (Sure, let's go.)
(No, let's get coffee at McDonald's.)

Part D. *Wh + Shall*

Chen: Where shall we go?
Bill: Let's try the gift shop.

Generalization

Wh questions for suggestions use *shall*.

Example: What shall we do?
Where shall we go?

---

1. T: Shall we go somewhere? — S: Where shall we go?
M1
Shall we walk somewhere? — Where shall we walk?
Shall we drive somewhere? — Where shall we drive?
Shall we stop somewhere? — Where shall we stop?
Shall we eat somewhere? — Where shall we eat?
Shall we sit somewhere? — Where shall we sit?

2. T: Shall we go downtown sometime? — S: When shall we go?
M1T
Shall we do something? — What shall we do?
Shall we call someone? — Who shall we call?
Shall we go somewhere? — Where shall we go?
Shall we have something to eat? — What shall we have?
Shall we buy something? — What shall we buy?
Shall we invite someone to dinner? — Who shall we invite?
Shall we have a party sometime? — When shall we have a party?

3. T: go on vacation — S1: Where shall we go?
M2
S2: Let's go (to New York).

buy some books
go for a walk
eat lunch
go shopping
stop for coffee
get some ice cream
sit down
get some tea
have a beer
have dinner

4. T: do — S1: What shall we do?
M2 — S2: Let's (have a party).

invite — S1: Who shall we invite?
S2: Let's invite the ELI students.

make
eat
buy
go
cook
play
sing
dance

5. It's Saturday night. You and your roommate are bored. Discuss what you want to do
C and suggest activities. Use *what*, *where*, etc. If you don't like a suggestion, say "no" and suggest something else.

SUMMARY DIALOGUE

A Hostess Gift

1. Chen: Bill, give me some advice, will you?

2. Bill: Sure, Chen. What's the problem?

3. Chen: I'm going to dinner at the Wilsons' and I need a gift. Any ideas?*

4. Bill: Buy something nice but inexpensive.

5. Chen: How many things are nice <u>and</u> inexpensive in this country?

6. Bill: Uh . . . not many, I guess. How much money are you going to spend?

7. Chen: Between $10.00 and $20.00.

8. Bill: Oh, no! Don't spend that much! Let's keep it under $10.00.

9. Chen: That's fine with me. How about a few suggestions?

10. Bill: My mother likes flowers. A few roses aren't too expensive. Or . . . buy some candy—everybody likes candy.

11. Chen: I don't know, Bill. Where do you buy things like that?

12. Bill: Try the gift shop in the Student Union. They have a lot of things.

13. Chen: Shall we go there now?

*Note that in informal speech the Subject and Auxiliary verb is often left off. In this case the verb as well: Do you have any ideas? Any ideas?

14. Bill: "We?" I have a class, you know.

15. Chen: Come on, Bill. I need your help. Come with me.

16. Bill: How about later this afternoon?

17. Chen: How about right now? The invitation is for tonight.

18. Bill: OK, OK, but I only have a few minutes.

(At the gift shop)

19. Bill: These coasters are nice.

20. Chen: Yeah, but the color's not right.

21. Bill: This is a pretty vase.

22. Chen: But who needs a vase?

23. Bill: How about a few candles? My mother loves candles. You know, on the dinner table.

24. Chen: Why do you want candles when you have electricity?

25. Bill: You don't like any of my ideas. Shall we just forget about the whole thing?

26. Chen: I'm sorry, Bill. Don't be angry. Your customs are different. I don't understand these gifts. They don't mean anything to me.

27. Bill: Oh, it doesn't matter. I'm not angry. But we're not getting anywhere. You still don't have a gift . . . Wait a minute. Don't you have anything from your country?

28. Chen: Yes, I guess so. I have a few paintings. Is a painting all right?

29. Bill: That's perfect. You don't need to buy anything.

30. Chen: Oh? Thanks, Bill. Thanks for your help. And thanks for coming.

31. Bill: It's OK, it's OK.

COMMUNICATIVE ACTIVITIES

1) **Discussion.** In your country, how do people entertain their friends? Are there special times during the year when people entertain more than others? Are there special occasions (such as a birthday) when people are invited? What do people do at parties (stand up/sit down; sing/dance/talk/play games)? Do people bring gifts to the host?

2) **Roleplay.** One student is a clerk in a (gift) shop, another is the customer. The customer finds out the price of several items, chooses and pays. The clerk explains about the prices, takes the money and counts back the change.

Note to teachers: Make up cards with different information for the players. Make sure the prices are locally realistic. The cards might look like this:

A (Customer)	**B** (Clerk)
a) Ask about candles.	a) Three large candles—$7.50
b) Ask about vases.	b) A small vase for 2 or 3 flowers—$4.95
c) Ask about candy.	c) 2 lbs. of chocolate—$9.75
Select the items nearest $10.	Try to convince A to take the candles.

Lesson Six
Fast Food

Introduction

Near the university there are many small restaurants. They sell "fast food." That is food which does not take a long time to prepare. Restaurants like these are popular among students and working people, especially at lunch time.

Carlos and Ali are returning to school. They were playing soccer in the park. They stop at a fast food restaurant for lunch.

Vocabulary

Nouns		*Verbs*	*Adverbs*	*Adjectives*
cheeseburger	milkshake	starve	always	chicken
Coke	order	try	pretty	chocolate
corner	pie		sometimes	crowded
cream	salad	*Expressions*	usually	fast
exit	sandwich			
hamburger	seat	a piece of (pie)	*Prepositions*	*Conjunctions*
hot sauce	table			
line	window		at	and
			on	or

SECTION ONE

Post-Nominal Prepositional Phrases

Vocabulary

Nouns		*Verbs*	*Prepositions*
block	mayonnaise	double	down
blue jeans	mustard	get	near
fish sandwich	onions	play	next to
guy	relish		
hair	restaurant		
lettuce	tartar sauce		

Ali: The place on the corner has good food.

Generalization

Single word modifiers (like *fat*) go before the noun; phrases (*in my class*) go after the noun.

Example: That fat guy in my class is really smart.

1. Rep: The restaurant on the corner has good food.
M1 Sub: near my house — S: The restaurant near my house has good food.
next to the bank — The restaurant next to the bank has good food.
two blocks down — The restaurant two blocks down has good food.
across the street — The restaurant across the street has good food.
near the university — The restaurant near the university has good food.

2. Rep: That tall guy is getting a hamburger.
M1 Sub: short — S: That short guy is getting a hamburger.
little — That little guy is getting a hamburger.
blonde — That blonde guy is getting a hamburger.
thin — That thin guy is getting a hamburger.
old — That old guy is getting a hamburger.
fat — That fat guy is getting a hamburger.

3. Carlos and Ali are talking in the restaurant.

M1T Rep: That tall girl with the long hair is going to have lunch with us.

Sub: thin	S: That thin girl with the long hair is going to have lunch with us.
short	That short girl with the long hair is going to have lunch with us.
in blue jeans	That short girl in blue jeans is going to have lunch with us.
pretty	That pretty girl in blue jeans is going to have lunch with us.
next to the door	That pretty girl next to the door is going to have lunch with us.
good-looking	That good-looking girl next to the door is going to have lunch with us.
with the funny hat	That good-looking girl with the funny hat is going to have lunch with us.
tall	That tall girl with the funny hat is going to have lunch with us.

4. Carlos and Ali get their order.

M2 Rep: I like the large cheeseburger with a lot of catsup.

Sub: small cheeseburger/lettuce	S: I like the small cheeseburger with a lot of lettuce.
plain hamburger/mustard	I like the plain hamburger with a lot of mustard.
chicken sandwich/mayonnaise	I like the chicken sandwich with a lot of mayonnaise.
fish sandwich/tartar sauce	I like the fish sandwich with a lot of tartar sauce.
beef hot dog/relish	I like the beef hot dog with a lot of relish.
double cheeseburger/onions	I like the double cheeseburger with a lot of onions.

5. What do you order when you go to a fast food restaurant?
C
Example: I like pizza with a lot of cheese and mushrooms.

6. You go to a fast food restaurant with your friend. Tell the person at the counter what you want. (Note: It is
C common to omit the subject and verb when placing an order.)

Example: A double cheeseburger with everything, a large Coke and an order of fries.

7. You are going to have dinner with a friend. S/he is waiting at the restaurant. You are fifteen minutes late. Tell
C the waiter.

Example: I'm looking for my friend. (He's a tall man with blonde hair.)
(She's a short girl with blue eyes and dark hair.)

SECTION TWO

Conjunctions: *and/or*

Carlos: I'm having pie and coffee. How about you?
Ali: I don't know. Just coffee or tea, maybe.

Generalization

The conjunctions *and/or* join words or sentences. *And* means an addition of items; *or* means you have choice of items.

---

1. Rep: He's getting a hamburger and a Coke.
M1 Sub: a sandwich and a Coke
coffee and ice cream
tea and toast
a cheeseburger and a milkshake
chicken and fries
bacon and eggs

2.
M1

T:	S:
go today/tomorrow	Shall we go today or tomorrow?
go with Nancy/Chen	Shall we go with Nancy or Chen?
go to McDonald's/Wendy's	Shall we go to McDonald's or Wendy's?
take the bus/a taxi	Shall we take the bus or a taxi?
order steak/chicken	Shall we order steak or chicken?
have pie/cake	Shall we have pie or cake?
drink tea/coffee	Shall we drink tea or coffee?

3. Maria is eating at her table. What is she having?
M2

T:	S:
pie/cake	She's having pie or cake.
a hamburger/a Coke	She's having a hamburger and a Coke.
tea/coffee	
a cheeseburger/fries	
breakfast/lunch	
a sandwich/a steak	
a milkshake/a Coke	
steak/potatoes	
pie/coffee	
a hot dog/a sandwich	

4. **M2** You're going to the fast food place to get lunch for everyone in the class. You have to remember the order.

T: I'm going to get a hamburger.

S1: I'm going to get a hamburger and (a steak sandwich).
S2: I'm going to get a hamburger and a steak sandwich and (a hot dog).
S3: . . .

5. **M2** T: She's getting a hamburger or ( ).
He's ordering coffee and ( ).
The food is cheap and ( ).
The boys are going downtown or ( ).
I want a steak sandwich and ( ).
Do you want a Coke or ( ).
Carlos is talking to Ali and ( ).
Is Ali buying a cheeseburger or ( ).
For dessert they're having ice cream and ( ).
After lunch the boys are going to the library or ( ).

S: She's getting a hamburger or (a cheeseburger).
He's ordering coffee and (pie).

6. **C** Ask your classmates. Ask your neighbor what s/he likes to eat in restaurants in his/her country.

Example: S1: What kind of food do you order in restaurants in your country?
S2: I like rice with beef or maybe fish in a hot sauce.

SECTION THREE

Frequency Adverbs

Ali: I *always* eat at this place.

Generalization

100% of the time	always usually often frequently
50% of the time	sometimes occasionally

	rarely	
	seldom	Negative
0% of the time	never	

Note: The percentages are only approximate.

Rarely, *seldom* and *never* are negatives and are not used when the verb is in the negative form.

Example: We don't often have pizza.
We rarely have pizza.

Part A. Statement with Affirmative Verb

1. Rep: We always eat at that place on the corner.
M1 Sub: sometimes — S: We sometimes eat at that place on the corner.
usually — We usually eat at that place on the corner.
often — We often eat at that place on the corner.
occasionally — We occasionally eat at that place on the corner.
never — We never eat at that place on the corner.
seldom — We seldom eat at that place on the corner.
rarely — We rarely eat at that place on the corner.

Generalization

Adverbs of frequency usually go before most verbs, but they come <u>after</u> the verb BE.

He always comes late.
He is always late.

Note: Sometimes, the adverb of frequency occurs in a different position.

Example: I eat there sometimes.
Usually it's not so bad.

---

2. Rep: He is never late for lunch.
M1 Sub: always — S: He is always late for lunch.
usually — He is usually late for lunch.
sometimes — He is sometimes late for lunch.
rarely — He is rarely late for lunch.
often — He is often late for lunch.
seldom — He is seldom late for lunch.

3. Negative Adverbs

M2 T: Do you often go out to lunch? S: I (rarely) go out to lunch.
I (don't often) go out to lunch.

Do you often eat fast food? S: I (seldom) eat fast food.
I (don't often) eat fast food.

Do you often buy a hamburger for lunch?
Do you often drink Coke?
Do you often go downtown for dinner?
Do you often have hot dogs?
Do you often put mustard on your hamburgers?
Do you often buy food to take home?
Do you often have a milkshake with your lunch?
Do you often go out at night for food?
Do you often eat french fries?

Part B. *Wh* Questions: *How often?*

Carlos: How often do you come to this place?
Ali: I always come here for lunch.

Generalization

The *wh* question of frequency is *how often?*

Examples:

	Do you	[often]	come here to eat?	Yes, I often stop here on the way home.
[How often]	do you		come here to eat?	I come two or three times a week.

---

1. Rep: How often do you go out for lunch?

M1 Sub: eat fast food — S: How often do you eat fast food?
get hungry for hamburgers — How often do you get hungry for hamburgers?
have sandwiches for lunch — How often do you have sandwiches for lunch?
eat American food — How often do you eat American food?
buy ice cream — How often do you buy ice cream?
come here for breakfast — How often do you come here for breakfast?
eat in a restaurant — How often do you eat in a restaurant?

2. Maria is having lunch.

M2 T: She's having a steak sandwich for lunch.
S1: How often does she have a steak sandwich for lunch?
S2: She (rarely) eats steak sandwiches. (She always has a steak sandwich for lunch.)
She's eating a cheeseburger and fries for lunch.
S1: How often does she eat a cheeseburger and fries for lunch?
S2: She (seldom) eats a cheeseburger and fries for lunch. (She always eats a cheeseburger and fries for lunch.)
She's having a hamburger and a milkshake.
She's having a salad.
She's getting a fish sandwich.
She's drinking coffee with sugar and cream.
She's buying a hot dog and a Coke.
She's having a salad with her hot dog.
She's eating a chicken sandwich with her salad.
She's ordering a chocolate milkshake.
She's getting a large piece of pie.

3. Ask your classmates. Ask your neighbor about eating in restaurants in the U.S.A.

C *Example:* S1: How often do you eat in restaurants?
S2: (I always have lunch in a fast food place.)
S1: Do you usually have a hamburger?
S2: (I often eat two or three.)

SECTION FOUR

Indefinite Pronoun: *one*

Part A. Singular

Salesclerk: Do you want a large Coke, Sir?
Carlos: No, a small one, please.

Generalization

One can be substituted for any count noun. It may follow adjectives

Example: Give me a large one, please.

Also, *one* may occur with *this* and *that*.

Example: Give me that one.

---

1. Rep: What kind of burger do you want?
M1 I want the big one.
What size Coke do you want?
I want the small one.

2. What kind of sandwich do you want?
M1 Rep: I want the big one.

Sub:	S:
small	I want the small one.
large	I want the large one.
expensive	I want the expensive one.
cheap	I want the cheap one.
inexpensive	I want the inexpensive one.
little	I want the little one.

3. Carlos has 10 hot dogs for his friends.
M1 Rep: Give me the one with a lot of mustard.

Sub:	S:
a lot of catsup	Give me the one with a lot of catsup.
a little relish	Give me the one with a little relish.
everything	Give me the one with everything.
a lot of hot sauce	Give me the one with a lot of hot sauce.
no catsup	Give me the one with no catsup.
a little hot sauce	Give me the one with a little hot sauce.
no mustard	Give me the one with no mustard.
a lot of relish	Give me the one with a lot of relish.

4. Rep: Maria is having a large Coke.
M1 I want a small one.

Sub:	S:
hamburger	Maria is having a large hamburger. I want a small one.
cheeseburger	Maria is having a large cheeseburger. I want a small one.
chicken sandwich	Maria is having a large chicken sandwich. I want a small one.
milkshake	Maria is having a large milkshake. I want a small one.
hot dog	Maria is having a large hot dog. I want a small one.
order of fries	Maria is having a large order of fries. I want a small one.
glass of milk	Maria is having a large glass of milk. I want a small one.

5.
M1T

T:	S:
Ali is going to a new place.	He isn't going to an old one.
Carlos wants a cheap lunch.	He doesn't want an expensive one.
They are buying a big pizza.	They aren't buying a little one.
Please get me a small Coke.	Please don't get me a large one.
Maria's ordering an expensive lunch.	She's not ordering a cheap one.
She's drinking a large shake.	She's not drinking a small one.

6. T: hamburger
M2

hamburger	S1: (I want a big one. What kind do you want?)
	S2: I want a (small) one.
cheeseburger	S1: (I want a cheap one.)
	S2: (I want a cheap one, too!)
chicken sandwich	
pizza	
steak	
hot dog	
salad	
order of fries	
milkshake	
Coke	
hot dog	

7. Chain Exercise
M2 T: You're going to a fast food restaurant for lunch. Which one are you going to?
S1: I'm going to the one (downtown).
S2: (Hector) is going to the one downtown. I'm going to the (big one near the university).
S3: (Hector) is going to the one downtown. (Sabah) is going to the big one near the university. I'm going to the one (at the airport).

Part B. Plural—*Ones*

Carlos: Those large sandwiches are too expensive.
Ali: Try the small ones. They're cheap.

Generalization

The plural form *ones* may be used after adjectives.

Examples:
The large burgers — the large ones
The small sandwiches — the small ones

---

1. What kind of burgers do you like?
M1 Rep: I like big ones.

Sub:	S:
small	I like small ones.
thick	I like thick ones.
expensive	I like expensive ones.
cheap	I like cheap ones.
little	I like little ones.
large	I like large ones.

2. Maria likes large Cokes.
M1T Rep: I like small ones.

Sub:		S:
hamburgers		Maria likes large hamburgers. I like small ones.
milkshakes		Maria likes large milkshakes. I like small ones.
tuna sandwiches		Maria likes large tuna sandwiches. I like small ones.
cheeseburgers		Maria likes large cheeseburgers. I like small ones.
hot dogs		Maria likes large hot dogs. I like small ones.
pizzas		Maria likes large pizzas. I like small ones.
ice cream cones		Maria likes large ice cream cones. I like small ones.

3. T: hot dogs
M2

S1: (I like small hot dogs with mustard. What kind do you like?)
S2: (I like big ones with relish.)

pizzas

S1: (I like expensive pizzas with mushrooms. What kind do you like?)
S2: (I like expensive ones, too!)

steaks
hamburgers
breakfast
milkshakes
Cokes
sandwiches
salads
cups of coffee
desserts

SUMMARY DIALOGUE

Fast Food

1. Ali: You know it's about lunchtime?

2. Carlos: I'm starving.

3. Ali: Why don't we stop at the place on the corner.

4. Carlos: Is the food any good?

5. Ali: Not bad. I eat there sometimes. Let's try it.

They go inside.

6. Carlos: Is it always this crowded?

7. Ali: Usually it's not so bad. But they're pretty fast. See? There's a short line.

8. Carlos: What are you going to have?

9. Ali: I don't know. A hamburger or something.

10. Clerk: Can I take your order?

11. Ali: Yeah. Give me . . . uh . . . a cheeseburger and a chocolate shake.

12. Carlos: I'll take the chicken sandwich and a large Coke.

13. Clerk: OK. It'll be ready in just a minute.

14. Carlos: Where do you want to sit?

15. Ali: Let's take that seat next to the window.

16. Carlos: Which one?

17. Ali: There. The table near the exit.

18. Carlos: There's someone sitting there!

19. Ali: Yes. Her name is Maria.

20. Carlos: Let's go.

21. Clerk: Don't forget your order, sir!

COMMUNICATIVE ACTIVITIES

1) Discussion. Do people from your country eat out at restaurants frequently? On what occasions? Does the whole family go? Compare with your classmates what foods are eaten for the morning, mid-day and evening meals. What time, in general, are the meals eaten? (Note to teachers: discuss meal times in relation to climate and type and length of work day.)

2) Rejoinder—Polite Refusal "I don't think so."

A rejoinder is a reply in conversation. Sometimes it is a fixed expression with a specific meaning. Look at the examples:

A. X: We're having a bridge game. Are you coming?
Y: I don't think so. I have an exam tomorrow.
X: Maybe next time.

B. X: There's a great movie on. Let's go.
Y: I don't think so. Some friends are coming later.
X: Let's ask them, too.
Y: OK.

The phrase "I don't think so." + a reason is a polite way to refuse an invitation. Note: When you refuse an invitation it is always polite to give a reason. In A the reason is firm and X does not ask again. In B, however, the reason is not so serious and X asks again.
Problem. One student (A) invites another (B). B gives a polite refusal. A decides whether refusal is firm and continues the conversation.

Note to teachers: Cards can be made up for the students as suggested in Lesson 5.

Sample:	**A**	**B**
	Invite B to dinner. If B refuses firmly, respond to his refusal and quit conversation. If B doesn't refuse firmly, persist.	Refuse firmly.

Lesson Seven

The Football Game

Introduction

Yesterday there was an important game at the university. Chen was at Ali's apartment all afternoon. Ali and his friends were watching the game on television.

Chen doesn't understand this kind of football and he doesn't like it. Today he is talking to Bill about the big game.

Vocabulary

Nouns		*Verbs*	*Adjectives*
Africa	meter	sit	busy
apartment	month	watch	complicated
Asia	stadium	yell	stupid
business administration	touchdown		tired
computer science	vacation	*Expression*	whole
end zone	week	at ( )'s place	
Europe	weekend		*Idiomatic Expressions*
field goal	yard		keep score
game	year		kind of
			make sense

SECTION ONE

BE—Past Tense

Part A. Affirmative

Bill: Where were you yesterday?
Chen: I was at Ali's place. I was there the whole afternoon.

Generalization

I, he, she, it + *was*

We, they, you + *were*

---

1. Rep: I was in school yesterday morning.

M1 Sub: class — S: I was in class yesterday morning.
the library — I was in the library yesterday morning.
town — I was in town yesterday morning.
the lab — I was in the lab yesterday morning.
the park — I was in the park yesterday morning.
school — I was in school yesterday morning.

2. Rep: I was at Ali's place yesterday afternoon.

M2 Sub: he — S: He was at Ali's place yesterday afternoon.
she — She was at Ali's place yesterday afternoon.
my friend — My friend was at Ali's place yesterday afternoon.
Nancy — Nancy was at Ali's place yesterday afternoon.
everybody — Everybody was at Ali's place yesterday afternoon.
that guy — That guy was at Ali's place yesterday afternoon.

3. Rep: My friend was at home yesterday.

M1 Sub: I — S: I was at home yesterday.
at Ali's place — I was at Ali's place yesterday.
he — He was at Ali's place yesterday.
in school — He was in school yesterday.
Nancy — Nancy was in school yesterday.
at the party — Nancy was at the party yesterday.
she — She was at the party yesterday.

4. Rep: My friend and I were at home last night.

M1 Sub: at the party — S: My friend and I were at the party last night.
at Ali's place — My friend and I were at Ali's place last night.
at Bill's house — My friend and I were at Bill's house last night.
at my place — My friend and I were at my place last night.
at the restaurant — My friend and I were at the restaurant last night.
at the movies — My friend and I were at the movies last night.

5. **M1**	Rep:	My friend and I were in New York last weekend.	
	Sub:	we	S: We were in New York last weekend.
		they	They were in New York last weekend.
		my friends	My friends were in New York last weekend.
		Carlos and Chen	Carlos and Chen were in New York last weekend.
		you	You were in New York last weekend.
		you and your friend	You and your friend were in New York last weekend.
		those guys	Those guys were in New York last weekend.

6.	Rep:	We were excited about the game yesterday.	
M1T	Sub:	I	S: I was excited about the game yesterday.
		they	They were excited about the game yesterday.
		Ali	Ali was excited about the game yesterday.
		his friends	His friends were excited about the game yesterday.
		my friend and I	My friend and I were excited about the game yesterday.
		he	He was excited about the game yesterday.
		Mrs. Jackson	Mrs. Jackson was excited about the game yesterday.
		everybody	Everybody was excited about the game yesterday.

7.	Rep:	I was at the game last month.	
M1T	Sub:	Carlos and Ali	S: Carlos and Ali were at the game last month.
		at the party	Carlos and Ali were at the party last month.
		Nancy	Nancy was at the party last month.
		in New York	Nancy was in New York last month.
		my friend and I	My friend and I were in New York last month.
		at Bill's house	My friend and I were at Bill's house last month.
		we	We were at Bill's house last month.
		I	I was at Bill's house last month.

8.	T:	I/last week	S: I was (at the game) last week.
M2		Carlos and Bill/last month	Carlos and Bill were (in New York) last month.
		Chen/yesterday	
		Mr. Jackson/last night	
		( )/yesterday	
		we/last Friday	
		( ) and ( )/last weekend	
		she/yesterday afternoon	
		Mr. and Mrs. Jackson/yesterday	
		I/this morning	
		( ) and ( )/last year	
		Carlos/last June	

Part B. *Yes/No* Questions

Bill: Were you at the game yesterday?
Chen: No, I wasn't.

Generalization

The *Yes/No* questions for BE—past have the same formation as BE—present.

Examples:

Is he at the game today? Yes, he is. No, he isn't.
Was he at the game yesterday? Yes, he was. No, he wasn't.

Are they at home today? Yes, they are. No, they aren't.
Were they at home yesterday? Yes, they were. No, they weren't.

---

1. M1T

T:	S:
Ali is at the game today.	Was he at the game yesterday?
Ali is happy today.	Was he happy yesterday?
Nancy is at the stadium today.	Was she at the stadium yesterday?
Nancy is busy today.	Was she busy yesterday?
Nancy and Ali are busy today.	Were they busy yesterday?
Bill is at home today.	Was he at home yesterday?
Bill and Ali are tired today.	Were they tired yesterday?

2. M2

T: Ask (Ahmed) if he was at the game yesterday.
S1: Were you at the game yesterday?
S2: (Yes, I was.) (No, I wasn't.)
Ask ( ) if she was at home yesterday.
Ask ( ) if he was in the supermarket yesterday.
Ask ( ) if she was busy yesterday.
Ask ( ) and ( ) if they were at the game yesterday.
Ask ( ) if she was at home yesterday.
Ask ( ) if he was tired yesterday.
Ask ( ) and ( ) if they were late yesterday.
Ask ( ) if he was at a fast food restaurant yesterday.
Ask ( ) if ( ) and ( ) were at the cafeteria yesterday.
Ask ( ) if ( ) and ( ) were hungry yesterday.
Ask ( ) if ( ) was at the supermarket yesterday.

3. T: at home — S1: Were you at home (last night)?
M2 — S2: Yes, I was. I'm (always at home).

hungry in class — S1: Were you hungry in class (yesterday)?
S2: Yes, I was. I'm (always hungry in class).

in the cafeteria — S1: Were you in the cafeteria (in the morning)?
S2: No, I wasn't. I'm (never in the cafeteria).

in town
in school
in class
at the stadium
at home
at the game
tired after the game
at ( )'s apartment
hungry before the game
busy at home
downtown

4. T: Ask ( ) if ( ) was in New York last week.
C S1: Was ( ) in New York last week?
S2: I don't know.
(to S3) Were you in New York last week?
S3: (Yes, I was.)
S2: (Yes, she was.)
Ask ( ) if ( ) and ( ) were at the movies last night.
S1: Were ( ) and ( ) at the movies last night?
S2: I don't know.
(to S3 and S4) Were you at the movies last night?
S3:/S4: (No, we weren't.)
S2: (No, they weren't.)
Ask ( ) if ( ) was downtown last weekend.
Ask ( ) if ( ) was late for lunch last Saturday.
Ask ( ) if ( ) and ( ) were at the game last month.
Ask ( ) if ( ) was hungry this morning.
Ask ( ) if ( ) was busy at home last night.
Ask ( ) if ( ) and ( ) were at ( )'s place yesterday afternoon.
Ask ( ) if ( ) was at ( )'s party last weekend.
Ask ( ) if ( ) and ( ) were tired last Monday morning.
Ask ( ) if ( ) was hungry in class yesterday.
Ask ( ) if ( ) and ( ) were at the language lab last night.

Part C. *Wh* Questions

Bill: Who was there yesterday?
Chen: Ali was.

Generalization

The formation of *wh* questions is the same as in previous lessons.

With *who* the subject and verb are in normal order.

Example: Someone was at the game yesterday.
Who was at the game yesterday? Maria was.

1. **M2** T: Someone was in school yesterday.

S1: Who was in school yesterday?
S2: ( ) was.
S3: I wasn't in school. I was at the game.

Someone was at Ali's place yesterday.
Someone was at the game last Saturday.
Someone was at ( )'s party last weekend.
Someone was hungry in class yesterday.
Someone was in the cafeteria this morning.
Someone was in New York last weekend.
Someone was busy at home last night.
Someone was tired after the game yesterday.

Note: In *wh* questions with *where* and *when*, the subject and verb are inverted.

Examples:
Carlos was someplace yesterday.
Where were you yesterday? I was at home.

Carlos was at home sometime.
When were you at home? Yesterday.

---

2. **M2** T: ( ) was someplace yesterday.

S1: Where were you yesterday?
S2: (At home.)

( ) was someplace last night.
( ) was someplace last weekend.
( ) was someplace three days ago.
( ) was someplace yesterday afternoon.
( ) was someplace the day before yesterday.
( ) was someplace two hours ago.

3. T: late for class S1: When were you late for class?
M2 S2: (Last week.) (Never.)

sleepy in the lab
busy with the homework
at the game
downtown
in California
in Washington, D.C.
hungry in class
at the lab
at the movies
in the cafeteria
in the park

4. T: Were you ever in London? (When?)
C Where were you yesterday at 3:00?
When were you downtown?
Were you at a party last week? (Was it fun?)
Who was late for class last week? (Why?)
Was anyone absent last week? (Who?)
Were you ever late for a dinner invitation? (Why?)
Who was sleepy in lab last week?
Where were you last weekend?
When were you very tired? (Why?)
Who was very busy last week? (Why?)
Where were you at 9:00 this morning?

5. Situation: You are a police detective interviewing someone who is suspected of
C robbing a bank in Syracuse, New York, on May 12, 19—, at 2:15 p.m. Find out if the person was ever there, when, who he was with, where he was on the day of the robbery, etc.

Part D. Time Expressions—Answer to *When?*

Vocabulary

Season	*Day*	*Month*	
spring	Sunday	January	July
summer	Monday	February	August
fall (autumn)	Tuesday	March	September
winter	Wednesday	April	October
	Thursday	May	November
	Friday	June	December
	Saturday		

Bill: When were you at Ali's?
Chen: During the game.

Generalization

In answer to the question *When?* use in with general times ("in April"); use *on* with specific times such as dates or days ("on June 27"); use *during* to emphasize the length of time ("during the war").

In and *during* are used with the same expressions.

On preceding days and dates may be omitted:

"I was in Washington (on) June 23."

---

1. Situation: Bill was in California in 198-.
M1 Rep: I was in California in 198-.

Sub:	S:
April	I was in California in April.
the spring	I was in California in the spring.
June	I was in California in June.
198-	I was in California in 198-.
December	I was in California in December.
the fall	I was in California in the fall.

2. Rep: I was in London on Monday.
M1

Sub:	S:
June 27	I was in London on June 27.
Thursday	I was in London on Thursday.
April 29	I was in London on April 29.
July 20, 198-	I was in London on July 20, 198-.
Saturday	I was in London on Saturday.
my birthday	I was in London on my birthday.

3. Rep: I was in New York during 198-.
M1

Sub:	S:
summer vacation	I was in New York during summer vacation.
the summer	I was in New York during the summer.
the spring	I was in New York during the spring.
the fall	I was in New York during the fall.
198-	I was in New York during 198-.

4. T: California—198-
M1T
S1: When were you in California?
S2: I was in California in 198-.

California—June 12
S1: When were you in California?
S2: I was in California on June 12.

London—May	S1: When were you in London?
	S2: I was in London in May.
New York—1975	S1: When were you in New York?
	S2: I was in New York in 1975.
Chicago—February 23	S1: When were you in Chicago?
	S2: I was in Chicago on February 23.
Los Angeles—the summer	S1: When were you in Los Angeles?
	S2: I was in Los Angeles in the summer.
Florida—1979	S1: When were you in Florida?
	S2: I was in Florida in 1979.
Washington, D.C.—January 12	S1: When were you in Washington, D.C.?
	S2: I was in Washington, D.C. on January 12.
Pittsburgh—the winter	S1: When were you in Pittsburgh?
	S2: I was in Pittsburgh in the winter.
San Francisco—March	S1: When were you in San Francisco?
	S2: I was in San Francisco in March.

5. T: the spring
M2
Monday
June 25
198-
the winter
Saturday
the summer
November 23
September
Tuesday
January
the fall

S: (My country is beautiful in (during) the spring.)
(I always go to the library on Monday.)

6. T: When did you arrive here?
C
When does the next term begin?
When are you going to leave here?
When is your birthday?
Where were you on your birthday last year?
When is the weather nice in (country)?
Is the weather ever bad in ( )? When?
What date is your national holiday?
When is an important religious holiday?
What day do you usually do your shopping?
When does it rain a lot in ( )?
Does it ever snow in ( )? When?

S: (In June.) (On April 25.)

Part E. *How long?* and Time Responses

Bill: How long were you at Ali's?
Chen: All afternoon.

Note: Were you in New York [for a long time]?

[How long] were you in New York?

Generalization

When were you in New York?	In the summer. On August 15. During August.
How long were you in New York?	For three days.

Use the word *there* to avoid repeating the name of a place.

Example: I was there for three weeks.

1. T: Were you in London for a long time? S: How long were you in London?
M1
Were you in Chicago for a long time? How long were you in Chicago?
Were you in Florida for a long time? How long were you in Florida?
Were you in California for a long time? How long were you in California?
Were you in Los Angeles for a long time? How long were you in Los Angeles?
Were you in New York for a long time? How long were you in New York?
Were you in Europe for a long time? How long were you in Europe?
Were you in Asia for a long time? How long were you in Asia?
Were you in Africa for a long time? How long were you in Africa?

2. Rep: I was in London for two weeks.
M1T Sub: three months S: I was in London for three months.
two years I was in London for two years.
ten days I was in London for ten days.
a week I was in London for a week.
a month I was in London for a month.
a year I was in London for a year.

3. T: What city were you in last year? S1: (Paris.)
M2
S2: How long were you in Paris?
S1: I was there (for three weeks).

4. T: (Paris)—three weeks S1: How long were you in Paris?
M1T
S2: I was there for three weeks.
(Paris)—1975 S1: When were you in Paris?
S2: I was there in 1975.

(Paris)—April 5	S1: When were you in Paris? S2: I was there on April 5.
(London)—July 14	S1: When were you in London? S2: I was there on July 14.
(Caracus)—a month	S1: How long were you in Caracas? S2: I was there for a month.
(New York)—two days	S1: How long were you in New York? S2: I was there for two days.
(San Francisco)—June	S1: When were you in San Francisco? S2: I was there in June.
(Los Angeles)—May 3	S1: When were you in Los Angeles? S2: I was there on May 3.
(St. Louis)—two weeks	S1: How long were you in St. Louis? S2: I was there for two weeks.
(Boston)—December 31	S1: When were you in Boston? S2: I was there on December 31.
(Bangkok)—May	S1: When were you in Bangkok? S2: I was there in May.
(Mexico City)—my birthday	S1: When were you in Mexico City? S2: I was there on my birthday.
(New Zealand)—three years	S1: How long were you in New Zealand? S2: I was there for three years.

Note to teacher: Pick places the students have been.

5. T: Paris
C

Paris	S1: Were you in Paris (last year)? S2: (No, I wasn't.)
London	S1: Were you in London (last year)? S2: (Yes, I was.) S1: When were you there? S2: (In the spring.) (On April 12.) (During April.) S1: How long were you there? S2: (For three days.)
(Continue around the room)	

SECTION TWO

Past Continuous

Chen: I was at Ali's apartment.
Bill: Were you watching the game?
Chen: Yes. Ali and his friends were watching.

Generalization

Previous Pattern: I *am* watching TV now.
New Pattern: I *was* watching TV last night.

Formation of Past Continuous:

was/were + verb + *ing*

Usage: For an action at a specific time or a continuing action in the past.

Example: Chen was watching the game all afternoon.
Carlos and Chen were talking after class.

---

1. Rep: I was watching the game last week.
M1 Ali was talking to his friends.
He was sitting near the door.
We were eating pizza.
Ali's friends were talking about the game.
They were drinking beer.

2. Rep: I was watching TV at 10:00 last night.

M1

Sub:	S:
we	We were watching TV at 10:00 last night.
sleeping	We were sleeping at 10:00 last night.
11:00	We were sleeping at 11:00 last night.
yesterday	We were sleeping at 11:00 yesterday.
those guys	Those guys were sleeping at 11:00 yesterday.
studying chemistry	Those guys were studying chemistry at 11:00 yesterday.
2:00	Those guys were studying chemistry at 2:00 yesterday.
yesterday afternoon	Those guys were studying chemistry at 2:00 yesterday afternoon.
the boy	The boy was studying chemistry at 2:00 yesterday afternoon.
playing soccer	The boy was playing soccer at 2:00 yesterday afternoon.

3. **M1T**

T:	S:
I'm watching TV now.	Were you watching TV at the same time yesterday?
Jane is writing a letter now	Was she writing a letter at the same time yesterday?
Carlos is walking home now.	Was he walking home at the same time yesterday?

Chen and Nancy are waiting for a bus now.	Were they waiting for a bus at the same time yesterday?
Mrs. Jackson is watching the game now.	Was she watching the game at the same time yesterday?
Mr. and Mrs. Jackson are driving downtown now.	Were they driving downtown at the same time yesterday?
Bill is reading the newspaper.	Was he reading the newspaper at the same time yesterday?
Nancy is listening to the radio now.	Was she listening to the radio at the same time yesterday?
Ali and Carlos are playing soccer now.	Were they playing soccer at the same time yesterday?

4. Chain Exercise
M2 T: Yesterday at 6:00 I was watching the news What were you doing?

S1: Yesterday at 6:00 (Mr. Smith) was watching the news, and (I was eating dinner.) (to S2): What were you doing?
S2: Yesterday at 6:00 (Mr. Smith) was watching the news; (   ) was eating dinner; (I was working in the cafeteria.) (to S3): What were you doing?

5. T: Ask (   ) if he was watching the game at 2:00 yesterday afternoon.
M2
S1: Were you watching the game at 2:00 yesterday afternoon?
S2: No, I wasn't. I was (studying in the library).
Ask (   ) if he was watching TV last night.
Ask (   ) if he was playing soccer yesterday afternoon.
Ask (   ) if he was walking to school at 8:30 yesterday.
Ask (   ) if he was studying chemistry yesterday.
Ask (   ) if he was driving home at noon yesterday.
Ask (   ) if he was working in the Student Union yesterday.
Ask (   ) if he was taking a bus home yesterday afternoon.
Ask (   ) if he was walking downtown at midnight yesterday.
Ask (   ) if he was flying to London at noon last Saturday.
Ask (   ) if he was driving a Rolls-Royce yesterday afternoon.
Ask (   ) if he was reading the newspaper yesterday afternoon.
Ask (   ) if he was eating dinner at 3:30 yesterday.

6. T: What were you doing last night at midnight?
S: (Sleeping.) (Finishing my homework.)

C What was (   ) doing at 8:00 last night?
S1: I don't know. What were you doing at 8:00 yesterday?
S2: (Eating dinner.) (Watching TV.)

Where were you going at 8:30 yesterday morning?
What were you doing yesterday morning?

Exercise continues on next page.

Where were ( ) and ( ) yesterday morning?
What was ( ) doing at 4:30 yesterday?
Where were you going last Friday?
When were you studying reading yesterday?
When were you studying grammar yesterday?
When were you studying writing yesterday?
Were you doing your homework at 4:00 this morning?
Where were you at 9:00 yesterday?
When was ( ) in (city)?

SECTION THREE

Conjunction: *but*

Bill: Well, do you like football?
Chen: The other guys like it, but it's confusing.

Generalization

Like *and* and *or* the word *but* joins words together. Use *but* when you join things that contrast.

Example: The game was good but confusing.
Soccer is hard, but not confusing.

---

1. Rep: Her TV is small but expensive.
M1 Sub: apartment — S: Her apartment is small but expensive.
car — Her car is small but expensive.
camera — Her camera is small but expensive.
typewriter — Her typewriter is small but expensive.
bag — Her bag is small but expensive.
book — Her book is small but expensive.

2. Rep: Chemistry is OK but not exciting.
M1 Sub: math — S: Math is OK but not exciting.
business administration — Business administration is OK but not exciting.
physics — Physics is OK but not exciting.
English — English is OK but not exciting.
engineering — Engineering is OK but not exciting.
computer science — Computer science is OK but not exciting.

3. **M2**

T:	S:
Ali was getting a new radio or . . .	Ali was getting a new radio or (a new TV).
Chen was having pizza and . . .	Chen was having pizza and (beer).
The pizza was good but . . .	The pizza was good but (expensive.)
The apartment was old but not . . .	
They were going to watch the game or . . .	
The game is interesting but . . .	
They were having hamburgers and . . .	
I was going to sit by the window or . . .	
Ali's friends were drinking Coke and . . .	
I was tired and . . .	
Their TV was big but not . . .	

4. **C** Ask your classmates. Ask your neighbor for his/her opinion about sports in the USA.

Example: S1: What do you think about sports in the USA?
S2: (I like basketball and football.)
(Football is interesting but not very exciting.)
(I don't like football or baseball.)

SUMMARY DIALOGUE

The Football Game

1. Bill: Chen, where were you yesterday? Our team was on TV, you know.

2. Chen: Yeah, I know. I was at Ali's apartment.

3. Bill: Were you watching the game?

4. Chen: Yeah, sort of. Ali was watching. He likes it. And his friends were watching. They like it.

5. Bill: But you don't.

6. Chen: Well, it's so stupid. I was there the whole afternoon, but I still don't understand your kind of football. It doesn't make sense.

7. Bill: Well, the rules are kind of complicated.

8. Chen: But nothing happens. It's so slow. And how do you keep score?

9. Bill: Well, you get six points for scoring a touchdown. That's when you carry or pass the ball over the goal line.

10. Chen: What did the announcer mean when he said that one guy "ran for 95"? Was that 95 points? I know it wasn't the number he had on his shirt. That was 27. And why do you need to put your back in the end zone?

11. Bill: The "back" is the runner, you see. And I think "95" meant 95 yards. Remember, the back ran nearly all the way down the field, but he didn't score a touchdown.

12. Chen: What's a yard?

13. Bill: Like a meter.

14. Chen: Oh.

15. Bill: The score was three to nothing, remember, because . . .

16. Chen: Wait a minute. How did we get three points? Half a touchdown?

17. Bill: There wasn't any touchdown, Chen.

18. Chen: So, how do you get three points?

19. Bill: A field goal. You kick the ball over the goal.

20. Chen: I don't like your kind of football, Bill.

COMMUNICATIVE ACTIVITIES

1) **Discussion.** What is the national sport of your country? What other sports do people enjoy? Are they spectators or participants? Do men and women enjoy the sports equally? Is the team or individual performance most important?

2) **Problem.** The class wants to have a party to celebrate (the end of the term). Find out what facilities are available and the regulations concerning alcohol, food, decorations, closing time, etc. The cost is especially important to know. Note to teachers: organizing a real party with committees, etc. gives them a lot of practice in practical English.

Styles of Language

To the Student:

Probably you have noticed that you can understand the teachers in the classroom much easier than you can your American friends at a party. This is because people speak different styles of language in different situations. Think about how you use your own language. Do you speak in the same manner to your friends as you do to your teachers?

In formal situations, the language spoken is most nearly like the written language. In informal situations there are more contractions, words are omitted, and some verb tenses are not used.

The style you should use is the style taught in the classroom, but you should be able to understand a more informal style. Following are two conversations about the same topic in different styles. Your teacher will help you find the differences.

Variations on a Theme—No. 1

Last weekend Bill went to see a professional football game. The Washington Redskins were playing the San Francisco 49ers. He's discussing it with Nancy.

1. Nancy: Hey, Bill. What did you do over the weekend?
2. Bill: Went to the Redskins' game.
3. Nancy: Lucky you! How did the 49ers look?
4. Bill: You know the 49ers. Pass, pass, pass. That's all they do.
5. Nancy: The fans go for that flashy stuff. I like a good strong running game. Bill, I've got to go to class. See you later, OK?
6. Bill: Yeah, see you.

Variations on a Theme—No. 2

On the way home on the bus, Bill sits next to a woman who lives down the street. She is a good friend of Bill's parents.

7. Mrs. Cassetti: Did you have a pleasant weekend, Bill?

8. Bill: Yes, thank you. I studied quite a bit, but Sunday I took the afternoon off and went to the football game. Washington was playing San Francisco.

9. Mrs. Cassetti: Oh? Did you enjoy the game?

10. Bill: Yes. We won. Our team looked pretty good. Of course any team would look good against San Francisco. Do you follow the games?

11. Mrs. Cassetti: Not any more. But when I was your age I liked to go. I always enjoyed the half time activities. From my point of view the music and the color were the reason for going. I have to get off here. It was nice to see you again, Bill.

12. Bill: It was nice talking to you. Goodbye, Mrs. Cassetti.

To the Teacher:

The dialogues have been numbered separately by lines so that you can refer to "Dialogue A, line—and Dialogue B, line—" and direct the students that way, or have them call attention to the items in the same manner.

The differences in the dialogue versions are largely those of informal vs. formal because of the relationship between the speakers; for example, friends in the one case and friend of one's parents in the other. The main differences are as follows:

(*1*) Phonology

Line 1 should be read [wə jə du]. All unstressed forms of *you* in the informal variation 1 should be read as [yə]; *to* as [tə]. The whole exchange should be read rapidly and with all possible contractions.

(*2*) Morphology/Syntax

a. Note the omission of subject pronouns in lines 2, 5, 6.
b. *gotta* line 5; *have to* in line 11.
c. Informal parting in lines 5, 6: formal in lines 11, 12.

(*3*) Lexicon

Football Terms

Line 2: Redskins: name of the Washington, D.C. professional football team

Line 3: 49ers: name of the San Francisco team
(It refers to the famous discovery of gold in California in 1849.)

Line 4: pass: to throw the ball forward

Line 5: running game: advancing the ball by running with it

Line 11: halftime activities: the entertainment on the field during the halftime intermission

color: the entertainment aspects of the game
(cheers, music, etc.)

Informal Expressions

Line 1: hey: very casual word used to get someone's attention

Line 5: flashy: superficially impressive (In this case it refers to passing the ball too much.)

Line 6: yeah: informal *yes*

Version 2 is slightly more formal because of the sex and age difference and the length of acquaintanceship among the speakers. Also (as the students have pointed out) Bill and Nancy may be trying to impress one another. There is need of more information on line 10. Bill implies here that San Francisco has a weak team that offers no competition to the Washington team.

The procedures we follow are roughly these:

1. The teacher reads both versions with books closed.
2. The teacher reads both again with books open.
3. The students are asked to point out specific differences between the two versions.

We also have the variations on tape so that students can listen in the laboratory but we do not encourage them to practice the informal dialogue. Production of very casual forms has often led to needlessly awkward and inappropriate use of these forms.

Lesson Eight

The Telephone

Introduction

Chen was thinking of his friend in California. He decided to call him long distance. But he did not know his friend's telephone number. He dialed the operator and tried to find out the number.

Vocabulary

Nouns	*Verbs*	*Adjectives*	*Phrases*
biography	decide	strange	area code
character	dial	toll-free	dial direct
living room	disconnect		directory assistance
operator	explain	*Adverb*	long distance
	hang up	really	person-to-person
	happen		station-to-station
	move	*Preposition*	wrong number
	remind (of)	through	
	ring		
	try		
	use		

SECTION ONE

in/on/at + Place

Chen: My friend lives in California.

Generalization

Use *in* with states, cities, countries and towns.
Use *on* with streets, etc. when the house number is not given.
Use *at* with house numbers.

Note: Written abbreviations:

Avenue	Ave.	Place	Pl.
Street	St.	Square	Sq.
Boulevard	Blvd.	Circle	Cir.
Drive	Dr.	Road	Rd.

Note: Numbers in addresses are spoken in groups of two if possible:

25	= twenty-five	2535	= twenty-five thirty-five
139	= one thirty-nine	1137	= eleven thirty-seven
but 101	= one oh one (an exception)		

1. Situation: My friend lives in California.
M1 Rep: He lives in California.

Sub:	S:
Pennsylvania	He lives in Pennsylvania.
New York	He lives in New York.
Pittsburgh	He lives in Pittsburgh.
San Francisco	He lives in San Francisco.
Washington, D.C.	He lives in Washington, D.C.
the United States	He lives in the United States.
Iran	He lives in Iran.
Oakland	He lives in Oakland.
Penn Hills	He lives in Penn Hills.
Beaver Falls, Pa.	He lives in Beaver Falls, Pa.
Homer, New York	He lives in Homer, New York.

2. Rep: He lives on Centre Avenue.
M1

Sub:	S:
Baum Boulevard	He lives on Baum Boulevard.
Fifth Avenue	He lives on Fifth Avenue.
Meyran Street	He lives on Meyran Street.
Forbes Avenue	He lives on Forbes Avenue.
Jefferson Drive	He lives on Jefferson Drive.
Park Place	He lives on Park Place.

3. Rep: He lives at 115 Centre Avenue.
M1

Sub:	S:
225 Forbes Avenue	He lives at 225 Forbes Avenue.
2535 Fifth Avenue	He lives at 2535 Fifth Avenue.
101 Main Street	He lives at 101 Main Street.

Exercise continues on next page.

139 Jefferson Drive	He lives at 139 Jefferson Drive.
1137 Atwood Street	He lives at 1137 Atwood Street.
4756 Baum Boulevard	He lives at 4756 Baum Boulevard.

4. T: Where do you live? S: (In Oakland.)
C What is your address? (381 Jefferson Drive.)
What street do you live on?
Where does your family live? (city, country)
What is your friend's address?
Where does the President of the United States live?
Where does the leader of your country live?
Where is the ELI office?
Where does ( ) live?
What street does ( ) live on?
Do all your friends live in ( )?

SECTION TWO

Using the Telephone

Operator: What city are you calling?
Chen: San Francisco.
Operator: Dial area code 415, then 555-1212.

Note: Telephone numbers in the U.S. consist of a three-digit area code (used when calling long distance), a three-digit local area number and a four-digit specific "station" number. Thus a number in Pittsburgh might be:

area code 412 343-0165

Telephone numbers are spoken in groups, usually with each number spoken separately. A person calling the number above would say: "Area code four-one-two (pause) three-four-three (pause) oh-one-six-five." Large round numbers are sometimes spoken as wholes; thus: 621-3500 is sometimes read as six-two-one (pause) three five hundred.

In large organizations such as a business, or a university, each office has a separate extension. This number is indicated by Ext. and another number.

XYZ Corporation	621-3500
Production Department	621-3500 Ext. 6562

Part A. Blackboard Exercise: Numbers

1. Rep: 624-5900
M1
(401) 963-2456
834-9725
441-5134
731-3052
922-4893
343-0160
(412) 624-5900 Extension 6562

2. T: Dictation. Write the following:
M1T
(412) 321-4869
673-4695
883-0415
391-2600 Ext. 519
531-5065
471-3213
481-4476
991-1900
828-3027
281-5015

Note to teacher: Use locally accurate numbers.

3. T: Blackboard Exercise. Read the following:
M1T
621-3500
731-3052
391-2600 Ext. 519
(412) 321-4889
441-5134
922-4893
834-9725
991-1900
531-5065
621-3500 Ext. 6562
(607) 749-2216 Ext. 2

4. T: My number is 343-0160. What's your number?
C
S: My number is ( ). What's your number? etc.

Note: The *Yellow Pages* is a list of businesses and services in the local community. You can find almost anything available by looking in the index. For example, if you are in a new city and want to go to a nearby Italian restaurant, look in the section "Restaurants," find one with an Italian name, then look at the address.

Part B. Situations

Vocabulary

Nouns	*Verbs*	*Adverbs*	*Adjective*
bank	change	right now	absent
checkbook	expect	sometime	
fire	lose		
lighter fluid	report	*Idiomatic Expressions*	
message	steal	Bye	
poison	swallow	I'm sorry.	
raincoat		leave a message	
taxi		May I take a message?	
		Thank you.	
		You're welcome.	

---

1. Wrong Number

A: Hello.
B: May I speak to Bill Jackson?
A: You must have the wrong number. There's no Bill Jackson here.
B: I'm sorry.
A: That's OK
(Hang up and dial again.)

C: Hello.
B: May I speak to Nancy please?
C: You must have the wrong number.
B: Is this 695-4826?
C: No, it isn't.
B: I'm sorry.
C: That's OK
(Hang up.)

Note: Do not give your number to a person who has dialed incorrectly.

D: Hello.
B: May I speak to Jane please?
D: You have the wrong number.
B: Is this 483-6191?

D: Yes, it is, but there's no one named Jane here.
B: I'm sorry to have bothered you.
(Hang up. Ask Jane her telephone number or call the operator to find out if the number has been changed.)

2. Person Not In
E: Linguistics.
B: May I speak to Professor Paulston, please.
E: She's not in right now. May I take a message?
B: No, I'll call back. What time do you expect her?
E: Sometime after 10:00.
B: Thank you, I'll try then.

F: Hello.
B: May I speak to Judy, please.
F: She's not here. Do you want to leave a message?
B: This is Carlos. Will you ask her to call me back?
F: Sure. Does she have your number?
B: Yes, she does. Thank you.
F: You're welcome. Bye.
B: Bye.

3. Salesman
B: Hello.
S: Mr. Jackson?
B: Yes.
S: Mr. Jackson, I'm calling for the Rest Easy Company. I'm sure you'll be happy to have one of our salesmen who will be on your street this week stop in and show you our newest line of goods which is the finest money can buy east of the Pacific or west of the Atlantic.
B: Thank you, but I'm not interested. (Hang up.)

Part C. Practice

T: **1.** Call Directory Assistance and get the number for John Hastings at 215 Maple Avenue.
2. Call Directory Assistance and get the number for Judy Wilson on Meadow Lane in Los Angeles.
3. Call the operator and report that you have dialed long distance incorrectly.
4. Your baby just swallowed some lighter fluid. Call the operator and get the number for the Poison Control Center.
5. Call the operator and report a fire in your apartment.
6. Someone stole your car. Call the police.
7. You have to go to the airport. Call a taxi.
8. You lost your checkbook. Call the bank.
9. Call a department store and find out if they have London Fog raincoats.
10. Call the English Language Institute and leave a message that you are going to be absent from class tomorrow.

SECTION THREE

Simple Past Tense

Part A. Affirmative

Chen: I dialed the number and waited. But nothing happened.

Generalization

Present: dial
Past: dial*ed*

There is only one form of the verb in the past tense for both singular and plural subjects. The spelling is usually *-ed*.

Note: The *ed* has 3 pronunciations.

Listen: learned (d), walked (t), wanted (ed).

---

1. Listen: I call California every day.
M1 I called California yesterday.
He watches football every day.
He watched the game yesterday.
They need the telephone every day.
They needed the telephone yesterday.

2. T: If you hear a verb in the present, raise one hand; if past, raise two.
M1T

We watch the game.	S: (1)
We watched the game.	(2)
He calls California.	(1)
He called California.	(2)
She needed a telephone.	(2)
She needs a telephone.	(1)
They need some money.	(1)
We wanted some money.	(2)
She learned a new word.	(2)
We studied our textbook.	(2)
He talks to the operator.	(1)
I wait for the bus.	(1)
They waited for the professor.	(2)
We play soccer in the park.	(1)
She works in the cafeteria.	(1)
I dialed the number.	(2)

		T/S	
3. **M1**	T:	call a friend dial a number answer the telephone try the number	S: He called a friend. He dialed a number. He answered the telephone. He tried the number.
	T:	talk a long time smoke a cigarette watch the game walk home	S: They talked a long time. They smoked a cigarette. They watched the game. They walked home.
	T:	need a camera want a new TV disconnect the telephone wait for my friend	S: I needed a camera. I wanted a new TV. I disconnected the telephone. I waited for my friend.

Generalization: Usage

Previous Pattern: I was watching TV at 2:00 yesterday afternoon.
New Pattern: I watched TV yesterday afternoon.

Use the simple past when you do not want to emphasize the continuousness of the action.

---

4. **M1T**	T:	He calls home every day. She talks to him every night. We expect a call every week. He dials the wrong number every day. We change our number every month. She talks to the operator every day. I call them every year.	S: He called home yesterday. She talked to him last night. We expected a call last week. He dialed the wrong number yesterday. We changed our number last month. She talked to the operator yesterday. I called them last year.
5. **M1T**	T:	order a new TV watch the game at 2:00 try the number use the telephone at noon talk to my brother at 4:00 expect your call wait for your call at 6:00 change my number disconnect my phone	S: I ordered a new TV yesterday. I was watching the game at 2:00 yesterday. I tried the number yesterday. I was using the telephone at noon yesterday. I was talking to my brother at 4:00 yesterday. I expected your call yesterday. I was waiting for your call at 6:00 yesterday. I changed my number yesterday. I disconnected my phone yesterday.
6. **M1T**	Rep: Sub:	He practices in the lab every day. tomorrow yesterday	 S: He is going to practice in the lab tomorrow. He practiced in the lab yesterday.

Exercise continues on next page.

	every day		He practices in the lab every day.
	now		He is practicing in the lab now.
	at 2:00 yesterday		He was practicing in the lab at 2:00 yesterday.
	tomorrow		He is going to practice in the lab at 2:00 tomorrow.

7.	Rep: They play soccer every Monday.		
M1T	Sub: last Monday	S:	They played soccer last Monday.
	next Monday		They're going to play soccer next Monday.
	we		We're going to play soccer next Monday.
	yesterday		We played soccer yesterday.
	at 5:00 yesterday		We were playing soccer at 5:00 yesterday.
	every day		We play soccer at 5:00 every day.
	the boys		The boys play soccer at 5:00 every day.
	tomorrow		The boys are going to play soccer at 5:00 tomorrow.

8.	Situation: Carlos needs a lot of money for phone calls.		
M1T	Rep: I need a dollar every day		
	Sub: yesterday	S:	I needed a dollar yesterday.
	next Tuesday		I'm going to need a dollar next Tuesday.
	you		You're going to need a dollar next Tuesday.
	last week		You needed a dollar last week.
	every morning		You need a dollar every morning.
	she		She needs a dollar every morning.
	yesterday		She needed a dollar yesterday.
	next Friday		She is going to need a dollar next Friday.

Part B. Interrogative and Short Answers

Nancy: Did you get the operator?
Chen: Yes, I did.

Generalization

Previous Pattern:	He call [s] his friend every day.	(Short Answer)
	Do [es] he call his friend every day?	Yes, he does. No, he doesn't.
New Pattern:	He call [ed] his friend yesterday.	
	D [id] he call his friend yesterday?	Yes, he did. No, he didn't.

---

1. Rep: Did you call your friend last night?
M1 Sub: dial a number — Did you dial a number last night?
ask the operator — Did you ask the operator last night?
answer a question — Did you answer a question last night?
talk to your sister — Did you talk to your sister last night?
make a long distance call — Did you make a long distance call last night?
expect my call — Did you expect my call last night?
dial a wrong number — Did you dial a wrong number last night?

2. Rep: Did Bill talk to his friend in Washington?
M1 Sub: call — S: Did Bill call his friend in Washington?
friends — Did Bill call his friends in Washington?
Chicago — Did Bill call his friends in Chicago?
write to — Did Bill write to his friends in Chicago?
girlfriend — Did Bill write to his girlfriend in Chicago?
San Francisco — Did Bill write to his girlfriend in San Francisco?

3. T: He calls his friend every day. — S: Did he call his friend yesterday?
M1T She talks to her sister every week. — Did she talk to her sister last week?
They watch the game every Sunday. — Did they watch the game last Sunday?
I play soccer every weekend. — Did you play soccer last weekend?
She eats in that restaurant every month. — Did she eat in that restaurant last month?
I have lunch here every day. — Did you have lunch here yesterday?
They come here every year. — Did they come here last year?
I go to the game every weekend. — Did you go to the game last weekend?
He needs a new car every year. — Did he need a new car last year?

4. Short Answers—Negative
M1 T: Did the woman call? — S: No, she didn't.
Did the man leave a message? — No, he didn't.
Did the boys make a long distance call? — No, they didn't.
Did Nancy talk on the phone? — No, she didn't.
Did the phone ring? — No, it didn't.

5. Short Answers—Affirmative
M1 T: Did Nancy call her friend? — S: Yes, she did.
Did Mr. Jackson use the phone? — Yes, he did.
Did Ali and Carlos make a long distance call? — Yes, they did.
Did Chen talk to the operator? — Yes, he did.
Did the novel remind him of his friend? — Yes, it did.

6. T: call your friend . . . every day. — S1: Do you call your friend every day?
M2 S2: (Yes, I do./No, I don't.)
yesterday — S1: Did you call your friend yesterday?
S2: (Yes, I did./No, I didn't.)

buy a new telephone (every year/last year)
make a long distance call (every day/last week)

Exercise continues on next page.

use the telephone (every evening/yesterday evening)
talk to your sister (every weekend/last weekend)
watch football on TV (every Saturday/last Saturday)
play soccer in the park (every afternoon/yesterday afternoon)
come here with Ali (every month/last month)
have lunch here (every day/yesterday)
eat in that place (every morning/yesterday morning)

Note: Do not confuse the pattern BE + adjective and past continous with the simple past tense.

Lesson Seven:	I was late.	BE + Adj.
	I was trying to call my friend.	Past continuous
Lesson Eight:	I tried to call California.	Simple Past

---

7. **M1T** T:

T	S
He calls every weekend.	Did he call last weekend?
She's on the telephone every day.	Was she on the telephone yesterday?
They watch TV at night.	Did they watch TV last night?
He's tired every morning.	Was he tired yesterday morning?
They're sleepy now.	Were they sleepy yesterday?
She's late for work every afternoon.	Was she late for work yesterday afternoon?
They go to the game every year.	Did they go to the game last year?
He watches the football games on TV every Saturday.	Did he watch the football games on TV last Saturday?
She's hungry every morning.	Was she hungry yesterday morning?
He eats fast food every day.	Did he eat fast food yesterday?
They have dinner in the cafeteria every evening.	Did they have dinner in the cafeteria yesterday evening?

8. **M2** T:

T	S
call California last weekend	S1: (Did you) (Did ( )) call California last weekend?
	S2: (Yes, I did./No, I didn't. I called Mexico.) (Yes, he did./No, he didn't. He didn't call anyone.)
walk to school at 8:00 yesterday	S1: (Were you) (Was ( )) walking to school at 8:00 yesterday?
	S2: (Yes, I was./No, I wasn't. I was sleeping.) Yes, he was./No, he wasn't. He was having breakfast.)
late to class yesterday	S1: (Were you) (Was ( )) late to class yesterday?
	S2: (Yes, I was./No, I wasn't) (Yes, he was./No he wasn't.)

sick last week
finish the book yesterday
sleepy at midnight last night
watch TV last night
busy yesterday
sleepy yesterday
watch TV at 8:00 last night
play tennis last week
practice in the lab at 4:00 yesterday
call your family last month

Part C. Negative

Chen: The operator said something. I didn't understand it.

Generalization

Lesson Four:	He	calls every day.
	He doesn't	call every day.
Lesson Eight:	He	called yesterday.
	He didn't	call yesterday.

Listen: I don't study every day.
I didn't study yesterday.
He doesn't watch TV every day.
He didn't watch TV yesterday.

1. Rep: I didn't call my friend last week.
M1 Sub: he — S: He didn't call his friend last week.
last Friday — He didn't call his friend last Friday.
last week — He didn't call his friend last week.
we — We didn't call our friend last week.
last month — We didn't call our friend last month.
you — You didn't call your friend last month.
I — I didn't call my friend last month.

2. Rep: I didn't have lunch here yesterday.
M1 Sub: he — S: He didn't have lunch here yesterday.
last Friday — He didn't have lunch here last Friday.
last week — He didn't have lunch here last week.
we — We didn't have lunch here last week.
last month — We didn't have lunch here last month.

Exercise continues on next page.

you — You didn't have lunch here last month.
yesterday afternoon — You didn't have lunch here yesterday afternoon.

I — I didn't have lunch here yesterday afternoon.

3. **M1T** T: I called her yesterday. — S: I didn't call her yesterday.
She was at work. — She wasn't at work.
Chen was sleeping at home. — Chen wasn't sleeping at home.
He was late for school yesterday. — He wasn't late for school yesterday.
We watched TV last night. — We didn't watch TV last night.
I was talking on the phone. — I wasn't talking on the phone.
We were having a pizza. — We weren't having a pizza.
Ali talked to us on the phone. — Ali didn't talk to us on the phone.
Nancy waited for us at the cafeteria. — Nancy didn't wait for us at the cafeteria.

4. Negative Response—Alternatives.
M2 T: Who called (X) yesterday?
S1: (Y) called (X) yesterday. X: (Y) didn't call me yesterday. (Z) called me yesterday. (Y) called me last week.

When did ( ) call home?
S1: He called home (last night.)
S2: I didn't call home last night. (I called last weekend).

When did ( ) make the call?
Who was talking on the phone last night?
Where was ( ) last weekend?
Who was watching the game yesterday afternoon?
Where did ( ) watch TV last night?
When was ( ) at your place?
Who ordered the pizza?
How much money did ( ) need for beer?
How many people did ( ) invite to his/her place?
Who made the long distance call to ( ) last night?

5. Ask your classmates. Find out where your neighbor studied (or worked) before.
C
Example: Did you have a job in your county?
(Yes, I worked in the Ministry of Education.)
(No, I was a university student. I studied biochemistry.)

Part D. *Wh* Questions

Bill: What happened?
Chen: I called three wrong numbers.

Generalization

Previous Pattern A:	Someone	called last night.
	Who	called last night?
	Something	is confusing.
	What	is confusing?
Previous Pattern B:		Did you want something?
	What	did you want?
New Pattern:		Did you want someone?
	Whom	did you want?

Remember: When the *some* word is in object position, the subject and verb are inverted. The *wh* word for people is *whom* in formal styles. You will never hear it in casual speech where *who* is used for both the subject and object pronoun.

Formal	*Informal*
Who studied?	Who studied?
Whom did you call?	Who did you call?

1. T: Did you call someone? S: Who did you call?
M1

T	S
Did you call someone?	Who did you call?
Did you meet someone?	Who did you meet?
Did he watch someone?	Who did he watch?
Did she describe someone?	Who did she describe?
Did you ask someone?	Who did you ask?
Did they want someone?	Who did they want?

2. T:
M1

T	
You called someone.	Who did you call?
You needed someone.	Who did you need?
He watched someone.	Who did he watch?
She described someone.	Who did she describe?
You asked someone.	Who did you ask?
They wanted someone.	Who did they want?

3. T:
M1T

T	S
You called someone.	Who did you call?
Someone called home.	Who called home?
You needed someone.	Who did you need?
Someone needed a dollar.	Who needed a dollar?
Someone described the restaurant.	Who described the restaurant?
He wanted someone.	Who did he want?
Someone watched TV.	Who watched TV?
She asked someone.	Who did she ask?
Someone mailed the letter.	Who mailed the letter?
They dialed someone.	Who did they dial?
Someone finished the pizza.	Who finished the pizza?

4. **M2** T: ( ) called someone — S1: Who did ( ) call? S2: He called ( ).

When? — S1: When did he call him? S2: He called him (last night).

Someone watched the game on TV. — S1: Who watched the game? S2: ( ).

Where? — S1: When did (he) watch it? S2: ( )

Someone watched TV.—Where?
Someone talked to me on the phone.—When?
Someone used the phone for a long distance call.—When?
( ) invited someone to a party.—When?
Someone wanted a party at school.—When?
Someone ordered hamburgers for lunch.—Where?
( ) finished all the sandwiches.—How many?

7. **C** T: Find out when ( ) called long distance and what kind of call it was. — S1: When did you call long distance? S2: (Last week I called Venezuela.) S1: (Did you call person-to-person?) S2: (No. Station-to-station.)

Find out when ( ) called long distance and who dialed the number, ( ) or the operator.
Find out if ( ) ever called a wrong number long distance and what happened.
Find out who helped ( ) with his first long distance and who s/he called.
Find out when someone called ( ) long distance and who it was.
Find out when ( ) watched TV and if the program was good.
Find out when someone asked ( ) for advice and what the person wanted.
Find out when ( ) received a package and what it was.
Find out if ( ) needed some money and how much.

8. **C** T: When did you arrive (in Pittsburgh)? — S: (Last month.)

Did you call someone yesterday? Whom? When?
Were you late for class yesterday?
Where were you at midnight yesterday? What were you doing?
Where did you live in 1975?
What were you doing at 6:00 last night?
Did someone call you last week? Who? When?
Did you receive a package yesterday?
How much money did you need for the bus yesterday?
How often were you late for class last week?
Where did you walk yesterday?
What were you doing at the Student Union yesterday?

SECTION FOUR

Place and Time

Chen: I was watching TV at home last night. My friend called me from California at 11 o'clock.

Generalization

	Place	*Specific Time*	*General Time*
We watched TV	in the living room	at 4:00	yesterday.

Note: You may hear different orders, but you will not be wrong if you use this order.

1.	Rep:	We watched TV at home last night.		
M1	Sub:	in the Student Union	S:	We watched TV in the Student Union last night.
		in the living room		We watched TV in the living room last night.
		in the bedroom		We watched TV in the bedroom last night.
		in the kitchen		We watched TV in the kitchen last night.
		in my apartment		We watched TV in my apartment last night.
2.	Rep:	We cooked hamburgers at home last night.		
M1	Sub:	yesterday	S:	We cooked hamburgers at home yesterday.
		last weekend		We cooked hamburgers at home last weekend.
		yesterday afternoon		We cooked hamburgers at home yesterday afternoon
		the day before yesterday		We cooked hamburgers at home the day before yesterday.
		last night		We cooked hamburgers at home last night.
3.	Rep:	They mailed a letter at the post office yesterday.		
M1	Sub:	I	S:	I mailed a letter at the post office yesterday.
		pick up		I picked up a letter at the post office yesterday.
		package		I picked up a package at the post office yesterday.
		last week		I picked up a package at the post office last week.
		Carlos		Carlos picked up a package at the post office last week.
		mail		Carlos mailed a package at the post office last week.

Exercise continues on next page.

a letter	Carlos mailed a letter at the post office last week.
Monday	Carlos mailed a letter at the post office last Monday.

4. Rep: I was at a movie downtown last night.

M1T Sub: we	S:	We were at a movie downtown last night.
a football game		We were at a football game downtown last night.
in Oakland		We were at a football game in Oakland last night.
yesterday afternoon		We were at a football game in Oakland yesterday afternoon.
my friend		My friend was at a football game in Oakland yesterday afternoon.
at Ali's place		My friend was at Ali's place in Oakland yesterday afternoon.

5. T: ( ) is going to have lunch S: ( ) is going to have lunch (in the cafeteria today).
M2

( ) is going to make a telephone call . . .
( ) is going to mail a letter . . .
( ) and ( ) are going to cook . . .
( ) didn't finish his breakfast . . .
( ) was at a restaurant . . .
( ) invited us to a party . . .
( ) cooked dinner . . .
( ) watched the game on . . .
( ) cooked dinner . . .
( ) watched the game on TV . . .
( ) walked home to his/her apartment . . .

6. Situation: A friend has just arrived from your country and is curious about your routine in
C the United States.

T: eat lunch S: I eat lunch (in the cafeteria at noon).
write letters I rarely write letters.
watch TV
go to class
study English
cook dinner
have breakfast
wait for the bus
go shopping

SUMMARY DIALOGUE

The Telephone

1. Chen: It was really strange.

2. Bill: What happened?

3. Chen: Well, I was reading a novel in the living room about four o'clock. A character in the book reminded me of my friend in California, so I decided to call him.

4. Nancy: At four o'clock in the afternoon? That's expensive!

5. Bill: Why did you call then?

6. Chen: I didn't know it was expensive. But it's OK; the call didn't go through.

7. Nancy: Why not?

8. Chen: I dialed the operator and waited and waited and waited . . .

(The conversation between Chen and the operator.)

9. Operator: (local): Operator.

10. Chen: I want to call California.

11. Operator: Do you have the number, sir? You can dial direct.

12. Chen: I don't have the number. I have the name and address.

13. Operator: Is this a person-to-person call?

14. Chen: No, station-to-station.

15. Operator: What city is it?

16. Chen: San Francisco.

17. Operator: Dial area code 415, then 555-1212. It's a toll-free call. The California operator has the number. Then hang up and dial the number.

18. Chen: Thank you, operator. (He hangs up; then, he dials the California number.)

19. Operator: (California): Directory assistance. What city please?

20. Chen: San Francisco.

21. Operator: Yes, may I help you?

22. Chen: Please give me the number for Dan Talbert at 415 Madison Street.

23. Operator: How do you spell the name?

24. Chen: Talbert, T-A-L-B-E-R-T.

25. Operator: Thank you. One moment please. The number is 683-5210.

26. Chen: 683-5210. Thank you, operator.

27. Operator: You're welcome.

28. Chen: I dialed the number, but it was busy. I tried later, and a girl answered. It was a wrong number. The third time it rang and then a woman said, "the number you have dialed has been dis—" Something I didn't understand.

29. Nancy: Disconnected?

30. Chen: Yes, that's it. What does it mean?

31. Nancy: The number is disconnected. Your friend isn't using it.

32. Chen: Oh, I see. Maybe he moved. I'm going to write him a letter. How much do I pay for all the calls?

33. Bill: The information call and the disconnected number are free. Call the operator and explain about the wrong number and it's free, too.

Communication Notes:

Line 21: The Directory Assistance number for long distance calls is always the same. Just dial the area code first.

Line 33: Chen probably dialed a wrong number when the girl answered. The computerized telephone system makes some mistakes, but not very often. Make sure to call the operator if you call long distance and dial incorrectly. Also, check your monthly bill to make sure the computer has all your changes correct.

COMMUNICATIVE ACTIVITIES

1) Discussion. How does the phone system work in your country? Does everyone have a phone? If you move, how do you get a phone? Do you pay for a phone in a private home? Are there public phones that anyone may use? Do you use coins in a pay phone? How much does it cost to make a call? For what purposes is the phone used (business/social calls)? Is there a public list of all the numbers? How do you get someone's number?

2) Problems.

a) You are visiting a friend and want to make a long distance phone call. How can you find out what the charges are?

b) Find out the charges to call a friend in another city (country) at various times of the day and week. Report to the class.

c) Describe to your classmates your experiences getting a phone in the U.S.A.

Lesson Nine

At the Bank

Introduction

Chen is at the bank. He just opened a checking account. Now he is using it for the first time. He wants to deposit a check and withdraw some cash, too. He and Carlos are going to buy a car. They want to pay cash for it. Chen meets Nancy at the bank and asks her some questions.

Vocabulary

Nouns		*Verbs*	
bank	line	ask for	exchange
bank statement	loan	borrow	fill out
bill	million/thousand	cash	lend
checking account	official	close	open
credit card	savings account	deposit	pick up
dealer	slip		withdraw
deposit	teller		
form	withdrawal		

Adjective	*Idioms*	*Expressions*
crowded	broke (no money)	make out (a check)
	cuts class	student loan

SECTION ONE

Modal Verbs—I

Part A-1. *Can*—Affirmative

Clerk: You can cash your check here.

Generalization

Can is called a modal verb. It comes before the main verb of the sentence:

Chen has a bank account.
He can cash a check at the bank.

Can adds the meaning of "ability to do something." It has only one form for all persons (unlike BE and DO), and when it is used, the main verb is always in the simple form.

Can is used with both present and future time words, but not with past time:

I can go with you now/tomorrow.

---

1. Rep: Chen can cash his check.
M1 Sub: open a new account
fill out the deposit form
talk to the bank manager
ask for a personal loan
withdraw four thousand dollars
ask for a bank check
deposit the check in his account

S: Chen can open a new account.
Chen can fill out the deposit form.
Chen can talk to the bank manager.
Chen can ask for a personal loan.
Chen can withdraw four thousand dollars.
Chen can ask for a bank check.
Chen can deposit the check in his account.

2. Rep: Carlos can drive a car in the United States.
M1 Sub: Chen
Nancy
the boys
they
she
we
he
I

S: Chen can drive a car in the United States.
Nancy can drive a car in the United States.
The boys can drive a car in the United States.
They can drive a car in the United States.
She can drive a car in the United States.
We can drive a car in the United States.
He can drive a car in the United States.
I can drive a car in the United States.

3. T: open an account
M1T
cash a check
fill out the slip
make a deposit
make a withdrawl
wait in line
ask for a loan
pick up the money

S: I can open an account; I'm opening an account now.
I can cash a check; I'm cashing a check now.
I can fill out the slip; I'm filling out the slip now.
I can make a deposit; I'm making a deposit now.
I can make a withdrawal; I'm making a withdrawal now.
I can wait in line; I'm waiting in line now.
I can ask for a loan; I'm asking for a loan now.
I can pick up the money; I'm picking up the money now.

Part A-2. Negative

Chen: I can't cash this check at the university.

Note: The modal is not usually stressed in the affirmative:

I can [kn] drive. (The stress is on the main verb.)

In a negative sentence, the modal usually receives more stress:

I can't [kæn] drive.

The contraction is used in speech, the full form in writing.

Spoken Form	*Written Form*
I can't borrow the money.	I cannot borrow the money.

---

4. Listen: Bill can drive, I can't drive.
M1 Bill can get a loan, I can't get a loan.
Bill can wait here; I can't wait here.

5. T: Raise one hand for positive, two for negative.
M1T

T:	S:
I can go.	(1)
I can't go.	(2)
I can't drive.	(2)
I can drive.	(1)
I can type.	(1)
I can't type.	(2)
I can speak English.	(1)
Carlos can't speak Spanish.	(2)
Bill can't cash a check.	(2)
We can go downtown.	(1)
They can't have my money.	(2)

6. **M1T**

T:	S:
We can open an account.	We can't open an account.
He can withdraw a thousand dollars.	He can't withdraw a thousand dollars.
I can get a loan.	I can't get a loan.
They can fill out the form.	They can't fill out the form.
She can wait in line.	She can't wait in line.
You can pick up the money.	You can't pick up the money.

7. T: Tell me what you can and cannot do.
M2

T:	S:
drive a car—fly a plane	(I can drive a car; I can't fly a plane.)
speak (Spanish)—speak (Arabic)	(I can't speak Arabic; I can speak Spanish.)
watch TV—be on TV	
ride on a bus—drive a bus	

Exercise continues on next page.

build a house—buy a house
stop the snow—watch the snow
open an account—own a bank
make a telephone—make a telephone call
buy a VW—buy a Rolls-Royce
cook dinner—eat dinner
write a letter—write a book

Part A-3. Interrogative

Chen: Can I deposit this money here?

Generalization

The modal verbs form questions in the same way as the sentences with BE: by inverting the subject and verb.

Examples:

BE	He's	buying something here.	
Yes/No	Is he	buying something here?	Yes, he is.
Wh	What is he	buying?	A car.
Modal	He can	buy something here.	
Yes/No	Can he	buy something here?	Yes, he can. (No, he can't.)
Wh	What can he	buy?	A car.

---

8. T: He can cash a check. — S: Can he cash a check?
M1
She can deposit her check. — Can she deposit her check?
He can withdraw a million dollars. — Can he withdraw a million dollars?
We can make a deposit here. — Can we make a deposit here?
She can make a withdrawal. — Can she make a withdrawal?
He can understand the bank statement. — Can he understand the bank statement?
They can get a loan at the bank. — Can they get a loan at the bank?
We can ask for a thousand dollars. — Can we ask for a thousand dollars?

9. You're talking to a bank official.
M2 T: Ask if you can open a savings account.
S1: Can I open a savings account?
S2: (Yes, you can.) (Sure, first sit down and fill out this form.)

Ask if you can open a checking account.
Ask if he/she can help you with the bank statement.
Ask if you can cash a foreign check.

Ask if you can get a personal loan.
Ask if you can withdraw ten thousand dollars.
Ask if he/she can exchange (pesos).
Ask if you can get a credit card.
Ask if you can close your account.
Ask if you can borrow a thousand dollars.
Ask if he/she can lend you four thousand dollars.

Note: Borrow and lend are "one-way" verbs in English.

The one who takes—borrows.
The one who gives—lends.

Can I borrow a dollar? / Can you lend me a dollar? } Sure. Here. { Thanks. I'll pay you back tomorrow.

---

10. Rep: Where can I cash a check?
M1 Sub: Bill — S: Where can Bill cash a check?

Sub	S
Bill	Where can Bill cash a check?
get some money	Where can Bill get some money?
when	When can Bill get some money?
Carlos	When can Carlos get some money?
make a deposit	When can Carlos make a deposit?
where	Where can Carlos make a deposit?
Jane	Where can Jane make a deposit?
borrow a dollar	Where can Jane borrow a dollar?

11. Situation: You are talking to a friend.
M2 T: Ask ( ) where you can cash a check.

S1: Where can I cash a check?
S2: You can cash a check at (the bank on Fifth Street).

Ask ( ) when he can help you with the homework.

S1: When can you help me with the homework?
S2: I can help you (this afternoon).

Ask ( ) where you can borrow some money.
Ask ( ) where you can mail a letter.
Ask ( ) where you can buy some stamps.
Ask ( ) where you can get a good car.
Ask ( ) when he can go downtown.
Ask ( ) when he can lend you some money.
Ask ( ) where you can take the TOEFL test.
Ask ( ) when he can go to the game.

Part B-1. *Will*

Chen: What do I do with these forms?
Nancy: Take them to the counter. The clerk will help you.

Generalization

Will indicates an action in the future; there is an element of promise, determination or inevitability. The pattern for the formation of negatives and questions is the same as for *can*. Note the contraction *won't*.

Spoken Form		*Written Form*	
She'll	get the money.	She will	get the money.
She won't	get the money.	She will not	get the money.

---

1. Rep: She'll open the account tomorrow.
M1 They'll give you some checks tomorrow.
I'll get some money tomorrow.
He'll make a deposit.
We'll ask for a loan.

2. Rep: I'll cash the check next week.
M1 Sub:

Sub	S
he	He'll cash the check next week.
deposit	He'll deposit the check next week.
the money	He'll deposit the money next week.
they	They'll deposit the money next week.
get	They'll get the money next week.
the loan	They'll get the loan next week.
the day after tomorrow	They'll get the loan the day after tomorrow.
she	She'll get the loan the day after tomorrow.
pay	She'll pay the loan the day after tomorrow.
the bill	She'll pay the bill the day after tomorrow.
next Monday	She'll pay the bill next Monday.

3. T:
M1T

T	S
He'll go to the bank.	He won't go to the bank.
She'll cash the check.	She won't cash the check.
We'll spend the money.	We won't spend the money.
He'll do it.	He won't do it.
We'll get it.	We won't get it.
They'll take it.	They won't take it.
She'll spend it.	She won't spend it.
I'll buy it.	I won't buy it.

4. **M2** T: Will you go somewhere tomorrow?

S1: Yes I will.
S2: Where will you go?
S1: I'll go (to the bank).

Will you cash this check sometime?

S1: Yes, I will.
S2: When will you cash it?
S1: I'll cash it (this afternoon).

Will you go to the bank sometime?
Will you cash this check somewhere?
Will you get the money sometime?
Will you open an account sometime?
Will you make a deposit somewhere?
Will you ask for a loan sometime?
Will you open a checking account somewhere?
Will you ask someone for a loan?
Will you buy something with the money?

5. **M2** T: have the money

S1: Will you have the money (tomorrow)?
S2: (Yes, I will.) (No, I won't have it.)

ask for a loan

S1: Will you ask for a loan (next week)?
S2: (Yes, I will.) (No, I never borrow money.)

look at used cars
buy a new car
pay in cash
bring the money
write me a check
ask for a bank loan

6. **C** Ask your neighbor about making a trip home.

Example: Will you travel by plane?
When will you go?
How much money will you need for the trip?
Where (what countries) will you visit?

Part B-2. Request Form

Note: This request pattern is an alternate to the pattern in Lesson Five.

Lesson Five: Please open the door.
Lesson Nine: Will you please open the door?

---

7. Carlos and Chen are nervous about going to the bank.

M1	T:	Please sit down.	S:	Will you please sit down?
		Please wait in line.		Will you please wait in line?
		Please have your money ready.		Will you please have your money ready?
		Please hurry.		Will you please hurry?
		Please get the pen.		Will you please get the pen?
		Please write the check.		Will you please write the check?

8.	Rep:	Please don't be late.	S:	Will you please not be late?
M1		Please don't hurry.		Will you please not hurry?
		Please don't drive so fast.		Will you please not drive so fast?
		Please don't speak so fast.		Will you please not speak so fast?
		Please don't spend the money.		Will you please not spend the money?

9.	T:	Ask ( ) to sit down.	S:	Will you please sit down?
M1T		Ask ( ) to stand up.		Will you please stand up?
		Ask ( ) not to be late.		Will you please not be late?
		Ask ( ) not to drive so fast.		Will you please not drive so fast?
		Ask ( ) to be on time.		Will you please be on time?
		Ask ( ) to speak slowly.		Will you please speak slowly?
		Ask ( ) to have the money ready.		Will you please have the money ready?
		Ask ( ) to drive slowly.		Will you please drive slowly?
		Ask ( ) to find the checkbook.		Will you please find the checkbook?
		Ask ( ) to get some checks.		Will you please get some checks?
		Ask ( ) to bring some money.		Will you please bring some money?
		Ask ( ) to lend you a pen.		Will you please lend me a pen?

Part C. *Should*

Nancy: Chen, you shouldn't carry that much cash around.
Chen: But, Carlos and I are buying a car today.

Generalization

Should indicates that it is a good idea to do something, that to perform the action in the future is desirable.

Examples: My parents live in another city; I should write them every week.
Chen was absent from class; I should call tonight and give him the assignment.

The pattern is the same as *can* and *will.*

Spoken Form		*Written Form*	
She should	learn to drive.	She should	learn to drive.
She shouldn't	learn to drive.	She should not	learn to drive.

Think: (Where do we find *should*—before or after the main verb? How do we form the negative?)

---

1. Rep: Chen should open an account.

M1 Sub: I — S: I should open an account.
we — We should open an account.
she — She should open an account.
they — They should open an account.
he — He should open an account.
you — You should open an account.

2. Rep: I should ask for a loan.

M1 Sub: he — S: He should ask for a loan
be at the bank on time — He should be at the bank on time.
the girls — The girls should be at the bank on time.
go to school on time every day — The girls should go to school on time every day.
the student — The student should go to school on time every day.
pay the bill right away — The student should pay the bill right away.
I — I should pay the bill right away.

3. Rep: Nancy shouldn't spend all her money.

M1 Sub: buy a car — S: Nancy shouldn't buy a car.
take a lot of cash — Nancy shouldn't take a lot of cash.
borrow money — Nancy shouldn't borrow money.
spend all her money — Nancy shouldn't spend all her money.
keep money at home — Nancy shouldn't keep money at home.
buy an old car — Nancy shouldn't buy an old car.
carry a lot of money around — Nancy shouldn't carry a lot of money around.

4. **M1T** T: It is a good idea to pay bills on time. — S: You should pay bills on time.
It is not a good idea to be late for dinner. — You shouldn't be late for dinner.
It is not a good idea to drive fast. — You shouldn't drive fast.
It is a good idea to write home often. — You should write home often.
It is a good idea to do the homework every day. — You should do the homework every day.
It is not a good idea to forget appointments. — You shouldn't forget appointments.
It is a good idea to open a savings account. — You should open a savings account.
It is not a good idea to borrow a lot of money. — You shouldn't borrow a lot of money.

5. Tell what is a good idea in the following situations.

M2 T: I'm going to have a test Friday. — S: (You should study.) (You shouldn't go to the movies.)
It's raining. — (You should take your umbrella.) (You shouldn't go out.)

Exercise continues on next page.

It's snowing.
I borrowed ten dollars from Bill last week.
I want to cash a check.
I want to learn English.
He has a million dollars at his house.
Lots of children are playing in the street. I'm driving a car.

6. What is proper in the following situations?
M2 T: If you have a test, should you go to the movies? S: (No, you shouldn't; you should study.) (Yes, you should relax before a test.)
If you have a test, should you copy from your friend?
If you have a test, should you bring your book to class?
If you have a test, should you talk to your friend?
If you have a test, should you stay up all night?
If you need money, should you borrow it from a friend?
If you have a problem, should you stay in your room?
If you have a question, should you be quiet?
If you have a test, should you drink a lot of beer?
If you have a test, should you watch TV?
If you have an appointment, should you be late?

7. T: Tell some things you should/shouldn't do in the United States/your country.
C Tell the truth.
S: (You should learn to speak English) in the United States.
(You shouldn't be late for appointments) in the United States.
(You should write a thank-you note for an invitation) in the United States.
(You shouldn't be absent from class without calling the teacher.)
(In my country, you should learn to speak ( ).)

8. T: Using the modals *can, will, should,* make statements about the following situations.
M2 Bill is a very good student at the university. He gets good grades. His friend Jack is not a good student. He goes to parties every night and cuts class often. Professor Johnson is going to give a test on Friday.
S: (Jack should study.) (Bill can go to the movies, but he probably won't.)

Judy has lots of new clothes and always has lots of money. She lends money to her friends all the time. They sometimes forget to pay her back. At the end of the month she is sometimes broke.

9. A new student asks you for advice about banking.
C T: When should I open an account? S: (Right away.)
Where can I cash a foreign check? (You can try the Federal Bank.)
What kind of account should I get?
Who can I talk to about a banking problem?
Where can I get a credit card?
When will I get my check?
Where will my money be safe?
When should I buy a Rolls-Royce?

What kind of car should I buy?
Where can I get the money?
When will the bank open?
What can I do with a bank card?

SECTION TWO

Articles

Part A. *a/the*

Chen: We're buying a car.
Nancy: Do you have it yet?
Chen: No, the car is still at the dealers.

Generalization

As you have seen, all singular count nouns are preceded by a definite article *the* or an indefinite article *a/an*. The choice of article depends on the context. When you use a noun that has been mentioned previously, it is preceded by a definite article:

"I opened an account yesterday."
"The account is at National Bank."

---

1. **M1** Rep: He wants a good bank. — The bank on the corner is good.
He wants a cheap car. — The little VW is cheap.
He wants a nice apartment. — The apartment next door is nice.
He wants a new camera. — The camera in the window is new.

2. **M2** T: Chen opened an account. — S: (The account is at Mellon Bank.)
The boys are getting a loan. — (The loan is for two thousand dollars.)
They're going to buy a car.
Carlos is renting an apartment.
Bill is getting a new job.
Nancy is getting a student loan.
Ali is buying a new car.
Chen is making out a check.
Carlos is withdrawing a thousand dollars.
The boys are looking at a used car.

3. T: Tell where you live and describe it.
C

S: (I live in an apartment. It's near here. The apartment has three rooms and a bath.)
(I live in a room in the dorm. The room is large and pleasant.)

Part B. No Article/*the*
Activity/Object Words

Generalization

Words like *home, school,* etc. take the definite article *the* if they are an object, not if they are part of an activity:

go to school — Activity
The school is big. — Object

---

1. Rep: He goes to bed at 8:00. The bed is very comfortable.
M1 We have dinner at 6:00. The dinner last night was delicious.
I go to school every day. The school is near my house.
We're in class now. The class is in the new building.
I go home by bus. The home of our friends is next door.

2. T: Tell if the situation describes an object or an activity.
M1T

We go to church on Sundays.	S: Activity
The church on the corner is small.	Object
I'm going home now.	Activity
The home of the President is the White House.	Object
Our children go to the school around the corner.	Object
The school is very new.	Object
She's going to school next year.	Activity

3. Situation: You and your classmate go out for a meal with a professor.
C T: Where did you go for lunch? S: (We went to an expensive restaurant for lunch.)
How was it? (Oh, the lunch was OK, I guess. But the service wasn't so good.)
Where did you go for dinner?
How did you like it?
When did you go for breakfast?

How was it?
When did you go for coffee?
How did you like it?
Where did you go for dessert?
How was it?

SECTION THREE

other/another

Part A. *the other* + Singular Noun Phrase

Chen: Is this the right form?
Clerk: No, sir. Please fill out the other one.

Generalization

Other can be used between the definite article and the noun it modifies:

the other bank
the other man

Other can also occur with *one:*

The bank is closed; let's go to the other one.

---

1. Situation: This bank is expensive.
M1 Rep: The other bank has free checking.
Sub: is friendly — S: The other bank is friendly.
is open evenings — The other bank is open evenings.
has short lines — The other bank has short lines.
has good service — The other bank has good service.
offers a credit card — The other bank offers a credit card.
pays interest on checking — The other bank pays interest on checking.
gives you a bank card — The other bank gives you a bank card.

2. Inside the bank, only two tellers are working.
M1 Rep: One teller is talking; the other one is eating her lunch.
Sub: woman — S: One woman is talking; the other one is eating her lunch.

Exercise continues on next page.

busy/on the telephone	One woman is busy; the other one is on the telephone.
man	One man is busy; the other one is on the telephone.
friendly/unfriendly	One man is friendly, the other one is unfriendly.
teller	One teller is friendly; the other one is unfriendly.
slow/fast	One teller is slow; the other one is fast.
guy	One guy is slow; the other one is fast.
taking a break/smoking a cigarette	One guy is taking a break; the other one is smoking a cigarette.

Part B. *Another*

Chen: I made a mistake on this form. Can you give me another one?

Generalization

Another can modify an indefinite noun:

another bank
another girl

Another can also occur with *one:*

This bank is awful, let's go to another one.

---

3. Rep: This teller is slow; let's go to another one.

M1 Sub:	S:
line	This line is slow. Let's go to another one.
awful	This line is awful. Let's go to another one.
bank	This bank is awful. Let's go to another one.
terrible	This bank is terrible. Let's go to another one.
line	This line is terrible. Let's go to another one.
long	This line is long. Let's go to another one.

4. **M1** Rep: I made a mistake. Will you give another check?

Sub:	S:
form	I made a mistake. Will you give me another form?
slip	I made a mistake. Will you give me another slip?
check	I made a mistake. Will you give me another check?

green form	I made a mistake. Will you give me another green form?
white slip	I made a mistake. Will you give me another white slip?
piece of paper	I made a mistake. Will you give me another piece of paper?
blank check	I made a mistake. Will you give me another blank check?

Part C. *Other* + plural noun

Generalization

Other can occur with plural indefinite nouns.

Some banks are good; other banks are not so good.

5.
M1

T: Some banks are good (bad). — S: Other banks are bad.
Some lines are fast (slow). — Other lines are slow.
Some tellers are helpful (not helpful). — Other tellers are not helpful.
Some customers are friendly (unfriendly). — Other customers are unfriendly.
Some people are having lunch (working). — Other people are working.
Some people have checking accounts (savings). — Other people have savings accounts.
Some people are making withdrawals (deposits). — Other people are making deposits.
Some people are writing checks (paying bills). — Other people are paying bills.
Some tellers are going to lunch (coming back to work). — Other tellers are coming back to work.

6. Negative Reply
M2

T: Are all banks good? — S: No, some banks are good, other banks are (lousy).
Do all banks stay open in the evening? — No, some banks stay open. Other banks (close at 3:30).
Are all tellers friendly?
Are all banks busy?
Do all checking accounts give interest?
Do all banks open at 8:30 in the morning?
Are all checking accounts expensive?
Are all the customers unfriendly?
Does everyone borrow money?
Can everyone get a loan?
Should everyone get a credit card?
Does everyone keep (their) money in a bank?

7. Discuss banks in your country.

C T: Does everybody in (Columbia) keep (his) money in a bank?
Do the banks offer checking accounts?
Do people borrow money from the bank?
Are the bank tellers friendly?
Are the banks a safe place for money?
Do people save money?
Does the government control banks?
Are bank officials helpful?
Do people have checking accounts?
Are credit cards popular?
Does everyone use the banks?

S: (No, some people keep their money in a bank. Other people keep their money at home.)

SUMMARY DIALOGUE

At the Bank

Chen is at the bank. It's very crowded.

1. Chen: Excuse me, are you Nancy? My name is Chen. Do you remember me? We're in the same chemistry class.

2. Nancy: Sure I do, Chen. You look like you're in a hurry.

3. Chen: Yeah, I want to deposit this check and make a withdrawal, too.

4. Nancy: I didn't know you did your banking here.

5. Chen: I just opened a checking account. This is my first time. How can I deposit this?

6. Nancy: Just fill out a form.

7. Chen: This one?

8. Nancy: Unh-uh. The other one, the green one, is for deposits.

9. Chen: OK . . . let's see . . . checks . . . what's the check number?

10. Nancy: Oh, I don't know. Better leave it blank.

11. Chen: Will you hand me another form? I made a mistake.

12. Nancy: Here you go.

13. Chen: Can I put a withdrawal on this, too? On this yellow form?

14. Nancy: No, use the white one. You should sign it, too, Chen. Hey, is this right? I mean, I'm sorry, I didn't mean to look, but $4,000.00?

15. Chen: Sh . . . Not so loud! That's right. Carlos and I are buying a car.

16. Nancy: Chen, ask them to make out a bank check. You shouldn't carry that much money around.

17. Chen: But I'm just going to spend it.

18. Nancy: Don't take any chances.

Communication Note

Line 14. Why does Nancy apologize for looking at Chen's check?

COMMUNICATIVE ACTIVITIES

1) Discussion. In some countries the postal system is also used for banking. Discuss the similarities and differences in banking practices between your countries and the U.S.

2) Problems:

Note to teachers: You should take the part of the bank teller or manager if necessary. Divide the students into groups to decide how to express what they want to say. Then they can take turns being spokesman.

a) Go to the bank and open a savings/checking account. Find out charges, interest rates, etc.

b) Go to the bank and report the loss of your travellers' checks.

c) Call the bank to report the loss of your checkbook/savings account book.

d) You have received a notice from the bank that your checking account is overdrawn. You think it is because of a confusion of names with another foreign student.
   1) Call the bank and try to find out the difficulty.
   2) Go to the bank and straighten out the situation.

   Useful Vocabulary

overdrawn	social security number
insufficient funds	bounce a check (informal)

e) Homework Problem: Find out which local bank(s) have the best (cheapest) checking accounts and the best (highest interest rate) savings account. Report charges and interest rates to the class.

f) What is a "money machine"? Discuss the advantages and disadvantages of using a money machine card.

3) Discussion. Borrowing Things.

Customs regarding borrowing personal property vary from person to person. In general, its OK to borrow small things—a pencil, a light, a piece of paper (which is not usually returned), but many people don't like to lend personal things, such as combs. Among very good friends almost anything is borrowable, but should be returned in good condition in a short amount of time. Small amounts of money are lent among friends and should be repaid promptly.

In your country what items can be borrowed? What is the relationship among the people?

Lesson Ten

The Used Car

Introduction

Chen and Carlos bought a used car. They drove the car to a park, but it broke down. They got it fixed and went back to town. Ali saw them at the park and is telling Bill about their troubles.

Vocabulary

Nouns	*Verbs*	*Adjectives*	*Adverbs*
dealer	break down	East	real (informal)
disaster	fix	used	really
picnic	guess		up north
savings		*Expressions*	
state park	*Prepositions*	car trouble	
station wagon	outside of		
tools	over		

SECTION ONE

Irregular Past Tense—I

Part A. *Make, have,* and the vowel [ɔ]

Ali: They had car trouble.
Bill: But they just bought the car!

Generalization

The verbs in this group, except for *have* and *make*, have the vowel sound [ɔ] in the past tense.

Present	*Past*
make	made
have	had
teach	taught
think	thought
bring	brought
buy	bought
catch	caught

1. Rep: He had it.
M1 Sub: made — S: He made it.
bought — He bought it.
thought — He thought it.
brought — He brought it.
caught — He caught it.
taught — He taught it.

2. Rep: The boys had a lot of trouble.
M1 Sub: girls — S: The girls had a lot of trouble.
made — The girls made a lot of trouble.
money — The girls made a lot of money.
man — The man made a lot of money.
brought — The man brought a lot of money.
food — The man brought a lot of food.
bought — The man bought a lot of food.
boys — The boys bought a lot of food.

3. T: They have car trouble every day. — S: They had car trouble yesterday.
M1T He makes repairs every week. — He made repairs last week.
She brings her car to school every day. — She brought her car to school yesterday.
Carlos thinks about a new car every night. — Carlos thought about a new car last night.
Chen buys tools every month. — Chen bought tools last month.
Mrs. Jackson teaches English every summer. — Mrs. Jackson taught English last summer.
Nancy catches a cold every winter. — Nancy caught a cold last winter.

Part A-2. *Wh* Questions

Bill: When did they buy the car?
Ali: Last week. It's a big station wagon. I saw it at the picnic Saturday.

Generalization

Pattern A			*Pattern B*		
Wh word in Subject Position			*Wh* word in Object Position		
Present:	Someone	brings a picnic lunch.		He brings	something.
	Who	brings a picnic lunch?	Does	he bring	something?
			What does	he bring?	
Past:	Someone	brought a picnic lunch.		He brought	something.
	Who	brought a picnic lunch?	Did	he bring	something?
			What did	he bring?	

The formation of *wh* questions is the same as in Lessons Four and Eight. Try to answer the following questions without looking at the answers at the bottom of the page.

1. Which word indicates the tense in the statement?
2. Which word indicates the tense in the question?*

4. M2 T: Going on a picnic

make a picnic lunch	G1: Someone made a picnic lunch. G2: Who made a picnic lunch? S: (Mohammed) did.
bring a frisbee	G1: Someone brought a frisbee. G2: Who brought a frisbee? S: ( ) did.
buy hot dogs and Coke	G1: Someone bought hot dogs and Coke. G2: Who bought hot dogs and Coke? S: ( ) did.
catch the frisbee	G1: Someone caught the frisbee. G2: Who caught the frisbee? S: ( ) did.
make ice cream	G1: Someone made ice cream. G2: Who made ice cream? S: ( ) did.
think of a good game	G1: Someone thought of a good game. G2: Who thought of a good game? S: ( ) did.
teach us the game	G1: Someone taught us the game. G2: Who taught us the game? S: ( ) did.

*Answers to questions above.
1. The main verb (brings, brought).
2. The auxillary verb do (does, did).

5.	T:	Did he make something?	S:	What did he make?
M1		Did he think something?		What did he think?
		Did he bring something?		What did he bring?
		Did he buy something?		What did he buy?
		Did he teach something?		What did he teach?
		Did he have something?		What did he have?
		Did he catch something?		What did he catch?

6.	T:	They caught something.	S:	What did they catch?
M1T		They had something.		What did they have?
		They taught something.		What did they teach?
		They bought something.		What did they buy?
		They brought something.		What did they bring?
		They thought something.		What did they think?
		They made something.		What did they make?

7.	T:	I had a picnic sometime.	S:	When did you have a picnic?
M1T		I made sandwiches sometime.		When did you make sandwiches?
		I brought a frisbee sometime.		When did you bring a frisbee?
		I bought ice cream sometime.		When did you buy ice cream?
		I caught the frisbee sometime.		When did you catch the frisbee?
		I thought of a new game sometime.		When did you think of a new game?

8. Your class had a picnic.

M2	T:	Someone brought hot dogs.	S1:	Who brought hot dogs?
			S2:	(Julio) did.
		(Ahmed) brought something.	S1:	What did he bring?
			S2:	(Sandwiches.)
		( ) and ( ) made something.	S1:	What did they make?
		Someone bought a car.		Who bought a car?
		Someone had car trouble.		Who had car trouble?
		( ) had something.		What did ( ) have?
		( ) brought something.		What did ( ) bring?
		Someone thought of mustard.		Who thought of mustard?
		Someone taught us a new game.		Who taught a new game?
		( ) made something.		What did ( ) make?

9.	T:	He has car trouble every day.	S1:	Then he had car trouble yesterday.
M2			S2:	No, he didn't have car trouble yesterday.
			S1:	Why not?
			S2:	(He didn't drive.)
			S1:	When did he have car trouble?
			S2:	He had car trouble (last weekend).
		She brings a picnic lunch every weekend.	S1:	Then she brought a picnic lunch last weekend.
			S2:	No, she didn't bring one.
			S1:	Why not?
			S2:	(She was busy).

S1: When did she bring one?
S2: She brought one the week before last.

They have a picnic every Saturday.
She makes a lot of money every month.
He teaches auto repair every Wednesday evening.
They buy a new car every year.
She brings her car to school every day.
We catch a cold every winter.
He thinks about football every Saturday.

10. C T: Ask your neighbor how he/she adjusted to life in the U.S.A.

Example:

What did you bring with you from ( )? (I only brought traveler checks and some clothes.)
What did you buy here? (I bought winter clothes and a lot of books and food.)

Part B. Vowel [ɛ] in Past, Final Consonant Change

Every day Chen reads about used cars in the newspaper.
He read about one last night.

Bill: How much did it cost?
Ali: A lot. They got together and spent all of their money.

Generalization

The verbs in this group have the vowel [ɛ] or end in the consonant *t* or both in the past.

Present	*Past*	*Present*	*Past*
feed	fed	read	read (note change in pronunciation)
sleep	slept	spend	spent
lend	lent	send	sent
sweep	swept	leave	left
keep	kept	mean	meant
feel	felt	build	built

---

1. M1 Rep: He read it.
Sub: fed — S: He fed it.
swept — He swept it.
left — He left it.

Exercise continues on next page.

	kept		He kept it.
	meant		He meant it.
	felt		He felt it.
	lent		He lent it.
	sent		He sent it.
	spent		He spent it.

2. Rep: The boys lent a lot of money last week.
M1 Sub: books — S: The boys lent a lot of books last week.

read	The boys read a lot of books last week.
magazines	The boys read a lot of magazines last week.
kept	The boys kept a lot of magazines last week.
letters	The boys kept a lot of letters last week.
sent	The boys sent a lot of letters last week.

3. M1T

T:	S:
Nancy reads the newspaper during breakfast every morning.	She read the newspaper during breakfast yesterday morning.
She sweeps the floor of her apartment every day.	She swept the floor of her apartment yesterday.
She spends fifty dollars on bus fare every month.	She spent fifty dollars on bus fare last month.
She lends ten dollars to her roommate every week.	She lent ten dollars to her roommate last week.
She sends a check to the landlord every month.	She sent a check to the landlord last month.
She feeds leftovers to her cat every night.	She fed leftovers to her cat last night.
She leaves her place at eight o'clock every morning.	She left her place at eight o'clock yesterday morning.
She meets Ali for lunch every Tuesday.	She met Ali for lunch last Tuesday.

4. M2 T: read the newspaper

S1: Did you read the newspaper (yesterday)?
S2: No, I didn't. (I read it last week.) (I never read the newspaper.)

spend fifty dollars
sweep the floor
lend money to a friend
keep your money in a savings account in your country
send a letter home
read a good book
feel happy
sleep all morning
meet your friend for lunch
keep your appointment

5. M2 T: ( ) read something.

S1: What did he read?
S2: He read a (newspaper).

( ) met someone.

S1: Who did ( ) meet?

( ) spent some money.	How much money did ( ) spend?
( ) read something.	What did ( ) read?
( ) met ( ) someplace.	Where did ( ) meet ( )?
The boys met someone.	Who did they meet?
( ) and ( ) read something.	What did they read?
( ) spent some money.	How much money did ( ) spend?
Someone spent $10.00.	Who spent $10.00?
Someone swept the floor.	Who swept the floor?

6. T: When did you read the newspaper? S: (I read it this morning.)
C (Yesterday.)

How did you feel yesterday?
How long did you sleep last night?
When did you send a letter home?
Where did you keep your money at home?
How many books did you read last week?
How many letters did you send home last week?
Who did you meet during your first week here?
When did you leave your country?
Where did you meet your friend yesterday?
Who sent fifteen letters last week?

Part C. Unpredictable Past Tense

Ali: They found an old station wagon and bought it.
Bill: I told them they shouldn't buy a used car.

Generalization

There is no "rule" for these irregular past tense forms. Learn them in sentences.

Present	*Past*	*Present*	*Past*
find	found	say	said
hear	heard	tell	told
sell	sold	win	won
lose	lost	hold	held
stand	stood	sit	sat

---

1. Rep: I found it.
M1 Sub: said S: I said it.
heard I heard it.

Exercise continues on next page.

		told	I told it.
		sold	I sold it.
		won	I won it.
		lost	I lost it.
		held	I held it.
		stood on	I stood on it.
		sat on	I sat on it.

2. Rep: Chen was lucky; he found a good used car.
M1 Sub: unlucky; heard about the price. — S: Chen was unlucky; he heard about the price.
happy; sold his camera for two hundred dollars. — Chen was happy; he sold his camera for two hundred dollars.
unhappy; lost his money — Chen was unhappy; he lost his money.
lucky; won a hundred dollars in the lottery — Chen was lucky; he won a hundred dollars in the lottery.
unlucky; lost the ticket on the way downtown — Chen was unlucky; he lost the ticket on the way downtown.

3. T: find a dollar — S: We found a dollar.
M1T lose a book — We lost a book.
hear the news — We heard the news.
sell the car — We sold the car.
tell a lie — We told a lie.
win the game — We won the game.
say "hello" — We said "hello."

4. M1T

T:	G1:	T:	G2:
say	What did you say?	hello	I said "hello."
sell	What did you sell?	my camera	I sold my camera.
lose	What did you lose?	my keys	I lost my keys.
find	What did you find?	a good car	I found a good car.
win	What did you win?	the lottery	I won the lottery.
stand on	What did you stand on?	the chair	I stood on the chair.
sit on	What did you sit on?	the seat	I sat on the seat.
hear	What did you hear?	the news	I heard the news.

5. T: ask ( ) what he found; add a place — S1: What did you find (in the garage)?
M2 — S2: I found (my keys.)
ask ( ) what he lost; add a time — S1: What did you lose (yesterday)?
S2: I lost (my homework paper).
ask ( ) what he heard; add a time
ask ( ) what he bought; add a place
ask ( ) what he found; add a time
ask ( ) who he met; add a place
ask ( ) who he heard; add a place
ask ( ) who he found; add a time and place
ask ( ) how much he spent; add a time and place

ask ( ) how many telephone calls he made;
add a time

Review: Irregular Verb I

Present Tense Third Person Singular	*Past Tense and Past Participle**	*Others (unpredictable)*	
makes	made	find	found
has	had	lights	lit
teaches	taught	stands	stood
thinks	thought	understands	understood
bring	brought	says	said
buys	bought	hears	heard
catches	caught	tells	told
reads	read	sells	sold
meets	met	wins	won
feeds	fed	loses	lost
sleeps	slept	sits	sat
sweeps	swept	holds	held
leaves	left		
means	meant		
feels	felt		
lends	lent		
sends	sent		
spends	spent		
builds	built		

6. Chain Exercise
C What did you do last week?
Tell one thing. Use the verbs above.

Example: S1: I bought a record.
S2: ( ) bought a record, and I (read a book).
S3: ( ) bought a record. ( ) read a book. and I (found some money).

SECTION TWO

Compound Nouns

Ali: Nothing works in that car. Not the windshield wipers, not even the cigarette lighter.

*In Lesson Fourteen, you will study a verb tense which uses the past participle. Some irregular verbs have a special form for the past participle, but these do not. The past and the past participle are the same form.

Vocabulary

pencil sharpener*	windshield wiper
knife sharpener	fire extinguisher
coat hanger	lawn mower
can opener	record player
letter opener	room divider
dishwasher	pot holder
coffee maker	clothes dryer
rice cooker	hair dryer
paper cutter	
cigarette lighter	

Generalization

Previous Patterns: The tall girls are good students.

Lesson Ten: The English girls are history students.

When a noun (English, history) is in the same position as the adjective in the previous patterns, a compound noun results. Note that the stress pattern changes when there is a combination of two nouns. Listen carefully as your teacher pronounces the sentences.

1. M1

T:	S:
It opens cans.	It's a can opener.
It lights cigarettes.	It's a cigarette lighter.
It dries hair.	It's a hair dryer.
It washes dishes.	It's a dishwasher.
It makes ice cream.	It's an ice cream maker.
It dries clothes.	It's a clothes dryer.
It cooks rice.	It's a rice cooker.
It makes coffee.	It's a coffee maker.

2. MIT

T:	S:
He teaches English.	He's an English teacher.
She studies engineering.	She's an engineering student.
Ali drives a truck.	He's a truck driver.
She robs banks.	She's a bank robber.
He publishes newspapers.	He's a newspaper publisher.
She writes textbooks.	She's a textbook writer.

*Agent nouns are covered in Lesson Two. If the class began after that, you might want to cover the point briefly.

He counsels students. — He's a student counselor.
She smokes cigarettes. — She's a cigarette smoker.

3. **M2** T: sharpen—pencil
S1: (How can I) sharpen this pencil?
S2: (Use the) pencil sharpener (over there).

wash—dishes
S1: (How did you) wash the dishes (so fast)?
S2: (I used) a dishwasher.

sharpen—knife
hang—coat
wipe—the windshield
extinguish—the fire
cut—paper
mow—lawn
open—can
divide—room
make—coffee
cook—rice
dry—clothes

4. **M2** Chain
T: I'm going to the thrift store to get a rice cooker.
S1: ( ) is going to the thrift store to get a (rice cooker).
I'm going to get a (toaster).
S2: ( ) is going to the thrift store to get a rice cooker.
( ) is going to get a toaster.
I'm going to get a (hair dryer).

5. **C** Ask your neighbor. Do the people in your family have hobbies? What are they?

Example:
S1: Does anybody in your family collect things?
S2: (Oh, yes, my younger brother is a stamp collector.)
S1: How about sports?
S2: (I play soccer. My sister is volleyball player.)

SECTION THREE

Prearticles (Quantifiers)

Salesman: All of these cars are in good condition.

Generalization

Expressions of quantity go before the article and noun. Some expressions of quantity indicate a part of the quantity. If the context is clear, the article and noun may be omitted.

Example: My class has a lot of students.
Some of the students are from the United States.
Some are from Asia.

---

1. Rep: *Some* of the cars are used.
M1 *Five* of the cars are used.
A few of the cars are used.
Many of the cars are used.
A lot of the cars are used.
All of the cars are used.
Not many of the cars are used.

2. Rep: A few of the students are from the Middle East.
M1

Sub: three	S: Three of the students are from the Middle East.
professors	Three of the professors are from the Middle East.
Asia	Three of the professors are from Asia.
some	Some of the professors are from Asia.
cars	Some of the cars are from Asia.
the United States	Some of the cars are from the United States.
many	Many of the cars are from the United States.

3. Situation: Here are five Cadillacs and five Rolls-Royces.
M2

T: cheap	S: (Some of the cars are cheap.)
imported	(Half of the cars are imported.) (Five of the cars are imported.)
expensive	
made in the United States	
made in Great Britain	
ugly	

beautiful
little
economical
made in Canada

4. T: How many of the people in this class are from Iran? S: (Five of the people are from Iran.)
M2
How many of the people in this class are from Venezuela? (A few of the people are from Venezuela.)
How many of the people in this class are from (Colombia)?
How many of the people in this class are living in an apartment?
How many of the people in this class are from (Libya)?
How many of the people in this class are studying English?
How many of the people in this class have a car?
How many of the people in this class are graduate students?
How many of the people in this class commute to class?
How many of the people in this class live in the dorm?

Generalization

As you learned in Lesson Five, some expressions of quantity are used with count nouns, others with non-count nouns. The same is true of the prearticles.

Count

five
a few } of the pages
not many

Non-Count

a little
(not) much } of the money

Both kinds of Nouns

some
half
a lot } of the { pens / money }
all
none

---

5. Rep: Some of the money is from Mexico.
M1
A lot of the money is from Mexico.
Half of the money is from Mexico.
A little of the money is from the U.S.
None of the money is from the U.S.

6. Rep: Half of my money is in a savings account.
M1 Sub: some S: Some of my money is in a savings account.
a little A little of my money is in a savings account.

Exercise continues on next page.

	a lot	A lot of my money is in a savings account.
	not much	Not much of my money is in a savings account.
	all	All of my money is in a savings account.
	none	None of my money is in a savings account.

7. **M1T**	T:	A lot of the cars came from Asia.	S:	A few of the cars come from Asia.
		A lot of the pollution comes from big cars.		A little of the pollution comes from big cars.
		A lot of the gas comes from the Middle East.		A little of the gas comes from the Middle East.
		A lot of the students drive to school.		A few of the students drive to school.
		A lot of the drivers are reckless.		A few of the drivers are reckless.
		A lot of the trouble comes from young drivers.		A little of the trouble comes from young drivers.
		A lot of the young drivers are careful.		A few of the young drivers are careful.

8.	Rep:	Not much of the pollution is from Canada.		
M1T	Sub:	cars	S:	Not many of the cars are from Canada.
		money		Not much of the money is from Canada.
		people		Not many of the people are from Canada.
		gasoline		Not much of the gasoline is from Canada.
		drivers		Not many of the drivers are from Canada.
		oil		Not much of the oil is from Canada.

9. **M2**	T:	friends drive to school	S1:	(Do all of your friends drive to school?)
			S2:	(No, most of my friends take the bus.)
		friends study English	S1:	(How many of your friends study English?)
			S2:	(All of them.) (None of my friends study English.)
		friends like picnics		
		friends have cars		
		friends live in the dorms		
		friends borrow money for a car		
		friends have savings accounts		
		friends have credit cards		
		friends have U.S. drivers' licenses		

10. Discussion

Now that you have learned more about the United States, there may be some questions you want to ask. Use this pattern and ask the teacher.

S:	(Does it rain all of the time here?)	T:	(Not all the time, but in the spring it rains a lot.)
	(There are many big companies like U.S. Steel, American Oil, American Broadcasting Co. Does the government own some of the big companies?)		(No. The government doesn't own any of those companies.)

SECTION FOUR

was/were going to + Verb

Carlos: Chen and I were going to buy a new car, but we couldn't afford it.
So we bought a used car instead.

Generalization

Lesson Three: I'm going to study tomorrow.
Lesson Ten: I was going to study all day.

The pattern in Lesson Three indicates intentions of future activities.
The pattern in this Lesson indicates past intentions. It means that plans were changed.
The sentences are often combined with *but*, or *instead*.

I was going to buy a car but I'm going to buy a bicycle instead.
I was going to have a hamburger but I'm going to get Chinese food instead.
I wasn't going to stop in the cafeteria but I wanted a cup of coffee.

Note the difference between this pattern and the other past tenses you have studied:

Lesson Eight:	Simple Past	I studied yesterday.
Lesson Seven:	Past Continuous	I was studying at 8:00 last night.
Lesson Ten:	New Pattern	I was going to study last night, but I didn't.

---

1. Situation: I was going to study all weekend, but we went on a picnic.
M1 Rep: I was going to study all weekend.

Sub: we	S: We were going to study all weekend.
sleep	We were going to sleep all weekend.
all day	We were going to sleep all day.
Judy	Judy was going to sleep all day.
work	Judy was going to work all day.
all morning	Judy was going to work all morning.
you	You were going to work all morning.

2. Rep: When was the man going to fix your car?
M1

Sub: where	S: Where was the man going to fix your car?
drive	Where was the man going to drive your car?
take	Where was the man going to take your car?
why	Why was the man going to take your car?
when	When was the man going to take your car?
paint	When was the man going to paint your car?
use	When was the man going to use your car?
how	How was the man going to use your car?

3. If you hear a sentence which describes a completed action in the past, say "I did
M1T it"; if uncompleted, say "But, I didn't."

T:	S:
I was driving home.	I did it.
I drove home.	I did it.
I was going to drive home.	But I didn't.
I wrote home.	I did it.
I was going to write a novel.	But I didn't.
I was writing to John.	I did it.
I was going to sleep all day.	But I didn't.
I was working at midnight.	I did it.
I was going to read all night.	But I didn't.

4. Tell what happened.
M1T

T:	S:
I wasn't going to call him.	I called him.
I was going to write her.	I didn't write her.
We were going to play bridge.	We didn't play bridge.
They weren't going to pay the bill.	They paid the bill.
He wasn't going to fly to New York.	He flew to New York.
She was going to do the dishes.	She didn't do the dishes.
We were going to quit smoking.	We didn't quit smoking.
They weren't going to write the letter.	They wrote the letter.

5.
M1T

T:	S:
drive to New York/ drive to California	I was going to drive to New York. I am going to drive to California, instead.
buy a Rolls-Royce/buy a Datsun	I was going to buy a Rolls-Royce; I'm going to buy a Datsun, instead.
pay by cash/pay by check	I was going to pay by cash; I'm going to pay by check, instead.
open a savings account/open a checking account.	I was going to open a savings account; I'm going to open a checking account, instead.
walk to the bank/take the bus	I was going to walk to the bank; I'm going to take the bus, instead.
finish my homework/have lunch	I was going to finish my homework; I'm going to have lunch, instead.
make a sandwich/get a hamburger	I was going to get a sandwich; I'm going to get a hamburger, instead.
have a cup of coffee/drink tea	I was going to have a cup of coffee; I'm going to drink tea, instead.

6.
M2

T:	S:
We were going to buy a new car . . .	We were going to buy a new car, (but we bought a used one instead.)
I wasn't going to pay cash . . .	I wasn't going to pay cash, (but the dealer wouldn't take a check).
We weren't going to buy a Ford . . .	
We were going to buy a Rolls-Royce . . .	
We were going to pick up the car this morning . . .	

I was going to drive the car to school . . .
I wasn't going to get a garage for the car . . .
I was going to get a money machine card . . .
I wasn't going to open a checking account . . .

7. C T: Did you do everything you planned for last weekend? What did you do instead?

S: (Not everything. I was going to go to the zoo, but it rained.)
(Almost everything. I was going to finish my homework, but I didn't have time. I went to a party.)

Did anyone persuade you to do something that you planned not to do?

(Yes, I wasn't going to study but my roommate told me about a test in biology.)

8. C T: Tell about a time when you had some very important plans which you changed.

S: (I was going to become a teacher. I studied engineering instead.)
(I wasn't going to come here, but I changed my mind.)

SUMMARY DIALOGUE

The Used Car

1. Bill: Did you go anywhere over the weekend?

2. Ali: Yeah, you know that big state park just outside of Crafton?

3. Bill: Yeah.

4. Ali: Well, I drove up there with a friend. It's a real nice place. We went for a picnic. But guess who we met there?

5. Bill: I don't know. Who?

6. Ali: Chen and Carlos. They bought a car, a big station wagon.

7. Bill: They bought it together?

8. Ali: Un huh. They got together and spent all their savings, I guess. It's really an expensive car.

9. Bill: New?

10. Ali: Nope. Used. I told them they shouldn't buy a used car.

11. Bill: I knew Carlos was trying to buy a car, but he said he didn't have the money.

12. Ali: The two of them had enough. But it was a disaster. The car already broke down once.

13. Bill: What?

14. Ali: Yeah, on Saturday. They had a problem. They were working on it in the park.

15. Bill: Where did they buy the thing, anyway?

16. Ali: They got it from some used car dealer on the East Side. They paid cash for it. They had some kind of warranty.

17. Bill: I hope so. I don't think they'll get their money back. Is the car running now?

18. Ali: Yeah, they repaired it at the park. But they were really mad.

19. Bill: I'll bet they were swearing in three languages.

20. Ali: At least three. But it worked. They got it fixed and drove off.

COMMUNICATIVE ACTIVITIES

1) Discussion. What kinds of cars are favored in your country? Can people buy used cars as Chen and Carlos did? What problems are caused by cars for your country?. Do they make life easier for some people? Who?

2) Rejoinders—Expressing Surprise, Agreeing.

Remember a rejoinder is a reply used in conversations.
Look at the examples:

A. X: Where is Carlos from?
Y: I think he's from Mexico.
X: He's not from Mexico. He's from Ecuador.
Y: Oh really? I didn't know that.

B. X: Where is Carlos from?
Y: I think he's from Mexico.
X: He's not from Mexico. He's from Ecuador.
Y: Oh that's right. Pablo is from Mexico.

In A, Y has the wrong information and expresses surprise "Oh really?" In B, Y simply forgot where Carlos was from and agrees when reminded "Oh, that's right."

Practice.

T: Carlos and Chen/buy a new car
S1: Carlos and Chen (are buying) a new car.
T: surprise
S2: Oh really? (I didn't think they had the money.)
S1: (I saw Carlos on the way to the car dealer's.)

T: Carlos and Chen/buy a new car
S1: Carlos and Chen (bought a new car last week).
T: agreement
S2: Oh that's right. (Carlos said they had the money.)

T: (student) is from (country) . . . agreement
(student) is from (city) . . . surprise
( ) is going to be (an engineer) . . . surprise
( ) and ( ) are from ( ) . . . agreement
( ) is an (interesting) place . . . surprise
( ) speaks (language) . . . surprise
( ) drives (a Rolls-Royce) . . . agreement
( ) went (to Paris for the weekend) . . . surprise

Note to teachers: Make up statements appropriate to your students' backgrounds and interests. Make sure the rejoinders are followed by some explanatory comment.

Lesson Eleven

Credit Cards

Introduction

Chen and Nancy are discussing credit cards. One of the large department stores offered a credit card to Chen. He wants to use it, but he is not sure how much it will cost. He doesn't want to pay too much interest on the monthly payments.

SECTION ONE

Irregular Verbs—II

Vocabulary

Nouns	*Verbs*	*Phrases*
bill	charge	cash or charge
charge slip	discuss	have a look (at . . .)
copy		it's up to (you)
credit	*Adjective*	on sale
credit card		per month
department store	convenient	what's the matter (with . . .)
fee		
interest		
manager		
percent		
sale		
videogame		

Part A. Affirmative

Chen: Nancy, did you see this?
Nancy: What is it?
Chen: A credit card. I got it from Kaufmann's. I took the card to the store, but the man spoke too fast.
Nancy: Maybe I can help.

IRREGULAR VERBS—II (All three parts different)

Third Person Singular—Present	*Simple Past*	**Past Participle*
is	was	been
gives	gave	given
eats	ate	eaten
drives	drove	driven
rides	rode	ridden
writes	wrote	written
drinks	drank	drunk
sings	sang	sung
rings	rang	rung
swims	swam	swum
throws	threw	thrown
knows	knew	known
grows	grew	grown
blows	blew	blown
takes	took	taken
goes	went	gone
does	did	done
sees	saw	seen
tears	tore	torn
wears	wore	worn
chooses	chose	chosen
speaks	spoke	spoken
breaks	broke	broken
wakes	woke	
gets	got	gotten

*The past participle is not used until Lesson Fourteen.

Generalization

These verbs, like those in Lesson Ten, have irregular past tense forms. They differ from the previous verbs in that there is a third part (Participle) which is different from the past and is used to form other tenses. The best way to memorize these irregular forms is to practice the sentences in Exercises 1–6.

		T:	S:
1.	T:	gave	S: He gave it.
M1		tore	He tore it.
		broke	He broke it.
		saw	He saw it.
		chose	He chose it.
		drank	He drank it.
		rang	He rang it.
2.	T:	wear	S: He wore it.
M1T		ring	He rang it.
		choose	He chose it.
		break	He broke it.
		give	He gave it.
		tear	He tore it.
		see	He saw it.
		drink	He drank it.
3.	T:	threw	S: I threw it.
M1		knew	I knew it.
		grew	I grew it.
		blew	I blew it.
		took	I took it.
		did	I did it.
4.	T:	She throws it.	S: She threw it.
M1T		She knows it.	She knew it.
		She does it.	She did it.
		She grows it.	She grew it.
		She takes it.	She took it.
		She blows it.	She blew it.
5.	T:	spoke	S: He spoke there.
M1		woke up	He woke up there.
		got	He got there.
		went	He went there.
		rode	He rode there.
		drove	He drove there.

ate	He ate there.
swam	He swam there.
wrote	He wrote there.

6. Situation: A day with Carlos.

	T:	S:
M1T	We wake up at 5:00 every day.	We woke up at 5:00 yesterday.
	We get up at noon every Saturday.	We got up at noon last Saturday.
	We ride a bicycle to work every morning.	We rode a bicycle to work yesterday morning.
	We drive my car to school every day.	We drove my car to school yesterday.
	We eat breakfast together every morning.	We ate breakfast together yesterday morning.
	We swim for an hour every afternoon.	We swam for an hour yesterday afternoon.
	We speak Spanish every evening.	We spoke Spanish yesterday evening.
	We see a movie every weekend.	We saw a movie last weekend.
	We write a letter to my parents every week.	We wrote a letter to my parents last week.

7. Situation: Ali in the U.S.A.

	T:	S:
M1T	He eats an apple every day.	He ate an apple yesterday.
	He gives money to his brother every month.	He gave money to his brother last month.
	He drives 10,000 miles every year.	He drove 10,000 miles last year.
	He rides his bike in the park every afternoon.	He rode his bike in the park yesterday afternoon.
	He drinks orange juice every morning.	He drank orange juice yesterday morning.
	He rings for the elevator every morning.	He rang for the elevator yesterday morning.
	He swims in the ocean every summer.	He swam in the ocean last summer.
	He sings in the shower every night.	He sang in the shower last night.
	He writes four letters every week.	He wrote four letters last week.

Part B. Questions

Nancy: Did they send you the card?
Chen: Yes, they did.

Generalization

Lesson Ten:	Affirmative:	She	sent the credit card.
	Yes/No Question:	Did she	send the credit card? Yes, she did.
	Wh Question:	When did she	send the credit card? Last week?
Lesson Eleven:	Affirmative:	He	took the card.
	Yes/No Question:	Did he	take the card? Yes, he did.
	Wh Question:	When did he	take the card? Last Saturday.

---

8. Situation: Life with Bill.

M1T T: He gives cash to the clerk every time.
S1: Did he give cash to the clerk last time?
S2: Of course he gave cash to the clerk last time.

He eats a steak every Saturday.
S1: Did he eat a steak last Saturday?
S2: Of course he ate a steak last Saturday.

He drives to work every Monday.
He rides his bicycle every Saturday.
He writes a letter every week.
He drinks milk for breakfast every day.
He sings in church every Sunday.
His alarm rings at 8:00 every morning.
He swims in the ocean every summer.
He sees a movie every week.
He takes a thousand dollars out of the bank every day.
He swims a mile every week.

9. Situation: Saturday afternoon activities.

M1T T: do the laundry/the dishes
G1: Did they do the laundry?
G2: No, they didn't do the laundry; they did the dishes.

break a dish/a glass
G1: Did they break a dish?
G2: No, they didn't break a dish; they broke a glass.

know the name of the theater/the name of the movie
see the movie/the play
wear boots/shoes
take a bus/a taxi
get good seats/bad seats
speak Spanish/English
go home/to a cafe
drink wine/coffee

10. Situation: Over the weekend.

M2 T: Someone drove a Rolls-Royce.
G1: Who drove a Rolls-Royce?
S1: ( ) did.
G2: When did he drive it?
S1: He drove it (Saturday).

Someone rode a bike.
G1: Who rode a bike?
S2: ( ) did.
G2: When did she ride it?
S2: She rode it ( ).

Someone wrote a song.
G1: Who wrote a song?
S3: ( ) did.
G2: When did he write it?
S3: He wrote it ( ).

Someone sang the song.
G1: Who sang the song?
S4: ( ) did.
G2: When did she sing it?
S4: She sang it ( ).

Someone ate a pizza.
G1: Who ate a pizza?
S5: ( ) did.
G2: When did he eat it.
S5: He ate it ( ).

Someone drank the beer.
G1: Who drank the beer?
S6: ( ) did.
G2: When did she drink it?
S6: She drank it ( ).

Someone gave a party.
G1: Who gave a party?
S7: ( ) did.
G2: When did he give it?
S7: He gave it ( ).

Someone broke a bottle.
G1: Who broke a bottle?
S8: ( ) did.
G2: When did she break it?
S8: She broke it ( ).

11. Situation: Chen's routine.

M2 T: He usually gets home at 10:00. (What time)?
S1: What time did he get home yesterday)?
S2: He got home at (9:00).

He usually wears a jacket (What?)
S1: What did he wear (last night)?
S2: He wore (an overcoat).

He usually goes downtown after class. (Where?)
He usually does his laundry on Saturday. (When?)
He usually eats four hot dogs. (How many?)
He usually takes a little money to school. (How much?)
He usually rides ( )'s bicycle. (Whose?)
He usually writes his parents. (Who?)
He usually wakes up at noon. (When?)
He usually sees his friend at the cafeteria. (Where?)

12. Chain exercise

C T: Use one of the verbs on page 207 and tell something you did last week.
S1: (I gave a lecture.)
S2: He gave a lecture and I (went to a party).
S3: He gave a lecture; she went to a party and I ( ).

13. T: What time did you wake up this morning?
S: (6:00.) (The alarm went off at 7:30.)

C
Who did you write to yesterday?
Where did you go last weekend?
When did you do your laundry?

Exercise continues on next page.

When did you see a good movie? Where?
Did you ever break your arm? How?
Did you ever see a movie star? Where?
How much money did you take on your trip? Where did you go?
How many people did you know when you came here? Who?
How often did you write home last week?
What time did you get home yesterday?
Did you get a letter yesterday?
Did you ever swim in the ocean? Which one? When?

SECTION TWO

here/there Adverbials

Part A. Location

Nancy: Did you use your card at the store?
Chen: I took it there. But I didn't use it.

Generalization

Here/there refer to the location of items in the same manner as the demonstrative adjective *this* and *that* (Lesson Three).

Here refers to something or someone near the speaker, and *there* far from the speaker.

Note that the pattern with nouns is different from the pattern with pronouns:

here/there	BE	Noun (Phrase)
Here	is	your credit card.
There	are	your keys.

here/there	Pronoun	BE
Here	it	is.
There	they	are.

When *here* and *there* are at the end of the sentence, they often have the form: *right here* or *over there*.

Example: I can't find my credit card. It's right here.
It's over there.

1.	T:	The book is on the table.	S:	There's the book.
M1		The hat is on the chair.		There's the hat.
		The car is on the corner.		There's the car.
		The store is down the street.		There's the store.
		The office is down the hall.		There's the office.
		The professor is near the door.		There's the professor.
2.	T:	The letters are on the desk.	S:	Here are the letters.
M1		The men are at the door.		Here are the men.
		The keys are in the lock.		Here are the keys.
		The girls are in the class.		Here are the girls.
		The books are on the table.		Here are the books.
		The papers are under the book.		Here are the papers.
3.	T:	There's the book.	S:	There it is.
M1		There's the man.		There he is.
		There's the girl.		There she is.
		There's the key.		There it is.
		There's the woman.		There she is.
		There's the letter.		There it is.
4.	T:	Here's the book.	S:	Here it is.
M1T		There's the key.		There it is.
		Here are the cards.		Here they are.
		There are the stores.		There they are.
		There's the girl.		There she is.
		Here's the woman.		Here she is.
		Here are the boys.		Here they are.
		There's the man.		There he is.
5.	T:	Where's your credit card?	S:	(Here it is.) (There it is.)
M2				(Here's my credit card.)
		Where are your papers?		(Here they are.) (There they are.)
				(There are my papers.)
		Where are ( )'s gloves?		
		Where is my book?		
		Where are my papers?		
		Where is ( )'s coat?		
		Where is ( )'s notebook?		
		Where are ( )'s books?		
		Where is ( )'s hat?		
		Where is your coat?		

Part B. Pronoun for place

Carlos: That store has good cameras.
Chen: Yeah. I was there this morning.

Generalization

Here and *there* substitute for places when the referent is known.

Examples:
Did you visit New York? Yes, I was there last month.
When will you see John? He'll be here next week.

1.	T:	Ali was in Tokyo last week.	S:	Ali was there last week.
M1		Ali was in Bombay last week.		Ali was there last week.
		Ali was in Thailand last week.		Ali was there last week.
		Ali was downtown last week.		Ali was there last week.
		Ali was in the country last week.		Ali was there last week.
		Ali was at the party last week.		Ali was there last week.
2.	Rep:	Bill will be here tomorrow.		
M1	Sub:	Bill and Chen	S:	Bill and Chen will be here tomorrow.
		next week		Bill and Chen will be here next week.
		the girl		The girl will be here next week.
		the day after tomorrow		The girl will be here the day after tomorrow.
		Nancy		Nancy will be here the day after tomorrow.
		the week after next		Nancy will be here the week after next.
		the men		The men will be here the week after next.
3.	On vacation			
M1T	T:	Bill was at the university last summer.	S:	Bill was here last summer.
		Chen will be in Asia next summer.		Chen will be there next summer.
		The boys will be in (New York) next spring.		The boys will be there next spring.
		Carlos was at school last weekend.		Carlos was here last weekend.
		Nancy was in Mexico last summer.		Nancy was there last summer.
		Ali will be at the university next spring.		Ali will be here next spring.
		Nancy will be in (California) next summer.		Nancy will be there next summer.
		Ali was in town last summer.		Ali was here last summer.
4.	T:	Bill wants to go to ( ).	S:	He can go there (next year).
M2		Maria wants to come to ( ).		She'll come here (next week).
		Chen and Nancy want to go to ( ).		
		I want to go to ( ).		
		( ) wants to visit ( ).		
		( ) wants to come to the U.S.		
		We want to visit ( ).		
		( ) and ( ) want to visit the class.		
		( ) and ( ) want to go to ( ).		
		( ) want to come to the university.		
		( ) and ( ) want to go to ( ).		
		( ) wants to come to our class.		

5. T: When is the best season to go to ( )? S: (You should go there in April. (That's carnival time.)
C
When is the worst time to go to ( )? (You shouldn't go there in December. The weather is cold.)

When is the best time to go to ( )? (People should come here in summer. In winter, it's awful.)

When should I visit ( )?
When should someone start school here?
When should someone not start school?

SECTION THREE

Modal Verbs—II

Nancy: A credit card? You ought to keep it. Of course, you have to pay interest, but it's worth it. You might see something you really want, and . . .
Chen: No, if I have to pay interest, I don't want it.

Part A. *Ought to**

Generalization

Ought to is a two-word modal that means *should* and like *should* precedes the simple form of the verb.

Example:
I should pay the bill. I ought to pay the bill.

Even though the modals have the same meaning, *should* is much more common in negative statements and questions:

Example:
Should we stay? Yes, we ought to.
No, we shouldn't.

---

1. Rep: I can go to the bank.
M1 Sub: should S: I should go to the bank.
will I will go to the bank.

Exercise continues on next page.

*This is presented mainly for recognition. Note that the students produce should.

	might			I might go to the bank.
	ought to			I ought to go to the bank.
	have to			I have to go to the bank.

2. T:	I ought to go now.		S:	I should go now.
M1	You ought to pay the rent.			You should pay the rent.
	He ought to open an account.			He should open an account.
	We ought to pay the bill.			We should pay the bill.
	She ought to do her work.			She should do her work.
	They ought to have a savings account.			They should have a savings account.
	I ought to study for the test.			I should study for the test.
	He ought to get a haircut.			He should get a haircut.

3. T:	We ought to go.	Question	S:	Should we go?
M1T	He ought to leave.	Negative		He shouldn't leave.
	They ought to pay the bill.	Question		Should they pay the bill?
	She ought to study.	Question		Should she study?
	You ought to buy a car.	Negative		You shouldn't buy a car.
	I ought to see my friend.	Negative		I shouldn't see my friend.
	He ought to write home.	Question		Should he write home?
	She ought to go to the movies.	Negative		She shouldn't go to the movies.

4. T: It's late. S: (I should go home.) (We ought to leave.)
M2 I have a test tomorrow. (I ought to study.) (I shouldn't go to the movies.)

I got a letter from my friend a month ago.
The professor doesn't like handwritten papers.
The house is quite dirty.
The professor gave an assignment for tomorrow.
Smoking is bad for people.
The gas tank is almost empty.
The grass is very tall.
The windows are dirty.
Big cars cause pollution.
My university is asking for money.
The bill is due in a few days.

Part B. *Might*

Nancy: You might see something really great.

Generalization

Might, which means possibility, indicates present or future time, depending on the context.

Examples: Maybe I'll go tomorrow
I might go tomorrow.

Maybe he is sick today.
He might be sick today.

As with the other modals, *might* precedes the simple form of the verb. *Not* is rarely contracted: I might not be on time.

1.	T:	Maybe I'll go to the movies.	S:	I might go to the movies.
M1		Maybe we'll stay home.		We might stay home.
		Maybe she'll study for the exam.		She might study for the exam.
		Maybe we'll go out.		We might go out.
		Maybe we'll get a pizza.		We might get a pizza.
		Maybe he'll buy a Coke.		He might buy a Coke.
		Maybe they'll walk home.		They might walk home.
		Maybe they'll be late.		They might be late.

2.	Rep:	I might not go to class today.		
M1	Sub:	go shopping	S:	I might not go shopping today.
		do the laundry		I might not do the laundry today.
		have the money		I might not have the money today.
		go home early		I might not go home early today.
		see John		I might not see John today.
		finish the lesson		I might not finish the lesson today.
		have time to do the assignment		I might not have time to do the assignment today.

3.	T:	Maybe Nancy is downtown.	S:	Nancy might be downtown.
M1T		Maybe Chen has some money.		Chen might have some money.
		Maybe they have a credit card.		They might have a credit card.
		Maybe their card is lost.		Their card might be lost.
		Maybe the store is expensive.		The store might be expensive.
		Maybe Nancy pays cash.		Nancy might pay cash.
		Maybe Chen is late.		Chen might be late.
		Maybe they have enough time.		They might have enough time.

4.	Homework			
M1T	T:	Maybe we won't finish on time.	S:	We might not finish on time.
		Maybe our friends will help us.		Our friends might help us.
		Maybe Ali will come early.		Ali might come early.
		Maybe Carlos won't come.		Carlos might not come.
		Maybe he's sick.		He might be sick.
		Maybe Chen will meet us here.		Chen might meet us here.
		Maybe we'll finish our homework.		We might finish our homework.
		Maybe Chen will do it for us.		Chen might do it for us.

5. Situation: Possibilities
M2 T: go to the park/the movies — S: (I might go to the park. I don't like movies.) (I might go to the movies. It's going to rain.)

eat at home/eat at a restaurant
have a hamburger/a salad
go to class/go home
write a letter/call my friend
study/watch TV
fix dinner/go out to eat
buy a newspaper/watch the TV news
have a cup of coffee/tea
do my homework/go to bed early
read a book/get a pizza

6. T: Tell something you might do next weekend. — S: (I might call my friend.)
C

Part C. *Have to*

Chen: Do I have to pay for the card?
Nancy: Not usually.

Generalization

Have to is somewhat different from the other modals; it agrees with the third person subject and has question and negative forms like the verb *have*.

Examples:	*Should* (etc.)	*Have to*
Statement:	He should leave	He has to leave.
Negative:	He shouldn't leave.	He doesn't have to leave.
Interrogative:	Should he leave?	Does he have to leave?
Answer:	Yes he should.	Yes he does.

Have to indicates a requirement or an obligation: We have to pay the rent.

---

1. Situation: Morning with Carlos
M1 Rep: I have to go downtown.

Sub:	S:
catch the bus	I have to catch the bus.
be on time	I have to be on time.
stop at the repair shop	I have to stop at the repair shop.
get my typewriter	I have to get my typewriter.
pay the bill	I have to pay the bill.
go to the bank	I have to go to the bank.
cash a check	I have to cash a check.

2. Situation: Chen's afternoon
M1 Rep: He has to study the lesson.

Sub:	S:
read the textbook	He has to read the textbook.
finish the homework	He has to finish the homework.
type the paper	He has to type the paper.
attend class	He has to attend class.
leave the building	He has to leave the building.
study in the library	He has to study in the library.
go to the post office	He has to go to the post office.
walk home	He has to walk home.
study for an exam	He has to study for an exam.

3. Situation: Nancy at school
M1 Rep: Does she have to go to class this afternoon?

Sub:	S:
finish the homework	Does she have to finish the homework this afternoon?
type a paper	Does she have to type a paper this afternoon?
talk to the professor	Does she have to talk to the professor this afternoon?
take an exam	Does she have to take an exam this afternoon?
go to the lab	Does she have to go to the lab this afternoon?
buy a textbook	Does she have to buy a textbook this afternoon?
study with Ali	Does she have to study with Ali this afternoon?
attend class	Does she have to attend class this afternoon?

4. Situation: On Saturday
M1 Rep: We don't have to go to school today.

Sub:	S:
do our homework	We don't have to do our homework today.
go to class	We don't have to go to class today.
be on time	We don't have to be on time today.
get up early	We don't have to get up early today.
type a paper	We don't have to type a paper today.
read the textbook	We don't have to read the textbook today.
study the lesson	We don't have to study the lesson today.

5. Situation: Chen and his credit card
M1T

T:	S:
go shopping downtown (possibility)	He might go shopping downtown.
apply for a credit card (good idea)	He should apply for a credit card.
pay 18% interest (obligation)	He has to pay 18% interest.
pay the bill on time (good idea)	He should pay the bill on time.
apply for two credit cards (possibility)	He might apply for two credit cards.
find a really good camera (possibility)	He might find a really good camera.
buy it on credit (obligation)	He has to buy it on credit.
talk to the manager (good idea)	He should talk to the manager.

6.
M2

T:	S:
I don't have to—	I don't have to (pay the bill until next week).
( ) has to— etc.	( ) has to take an exam today.

7. T: Ask ( ) when he has to pay the bill. S1: When do you have to pay the bill?
M2 S2: (Next week.) (I paid it yesterday.)

Ask ( ) when he has to cash a check.
Ask ( ) when she has to buy groceries.
Ask ( ) where he has to buy groceries.
Ask ( ) where she has to wait for the bus.
Ask ( ) where he has to cash a check.
Ask ( ) how often she has to go downtown.
Ask ( ) how often he has to cash a check.
Ask ( ) how often she has to use a credit card.

8. T: Tell something you have to do today and and when. S: (I have to go to the bank this afternoon.)
C
Tell something you don't have to do next weekend. (I don't have to study.)

9. Use a modal to comment on the following situations:
M2 T: Ali has a test tomorrow. His friends want him to go to the movies. S: (He should study.) (He shouldn't go to the movies.) (He ought to stay home.)

Jane is very fat. She wants to lose weight, but she loves candy.
It's raining. Bill has a headache. He also has a class at the university.
Bill needs some money for the weekend. It's 4:30; the bank closes at 5:00.
The bill just came from the university. (José) doesn't have the money to pay for it.
Chen just got a credit card. Kaufmann's is having a sale, but Chen doesn't have any money.
Someone stole Jane's wallet with all her credit cards.
In a large city you are totally lost.
You are in a bank when a robber comes in with a gun.
You finish dinner in an expensive restaurant and discover you don't have your wallet.
A good friend advises you to do something you think is wrong.

10. T: What do you have to do every day? S: (Get up at 6:00.) (Write to my girlfriend.)
C Why? (I'll be late.) (She'll get angry.)

What do you have to do if you're broke?
What are you going to do this weekend? (might)
What should you do if it's raining?
Do you have a credit card? How often do you have to pay?
Do you have to type your papers?
What are your plans for the weekend?
What are your plans for the summer?
Do you have to be on time to class? Why?
Are there things you have to do every day? What?
Are there things you ought to do every day? What?
Who ought to study very hard? Why?

SECTION FOUR

used to + Verb

Chen: I don't want to pay 18% interest.
Nancy: You won't if you pay the bill on time. I used to pay cash for everything, but now, I always go shopping with my credit card because it's so convenient.

Generalization

Used to + verb is a past expression which indicates something which was formerly a fact, but is no longer.

Example: I used to live in Boston; now I live in Pittsburgh.

---

1. Rep: I used to pay cash.
M1
Chen used to have a savings account.
We used to take the bus downtown.
Nancy used to park near the department store.
We used to have lunch together.
I used to shop at expensive stores.
Chen used to spend the whole day downtown.
He used to walk around the park.

2. T: I don't live in Boston any longer. — S: You used to live in Boston.
M1T
They don't have a VW any longer. — They used to have a VW.
He doesn't drive to work any longer. — He used to drive to work.
She doesn't smoke cigars any longer. — She used to smoke cigars.
We don't speak French well any longer. — You used to speak French well.
He doesn't study hard any longer. — He used to study hard.
They don't get up early any longer. — They used to get up early.
They don't come on time any longer. — They used to come on time.

3. T: I used to—, but now,—
M2
S1: I used to (live in Paris), but now I (live in the U.S.).
S2: I use to (have a VW), but now I (don't have a car).

4. T: Do you study the same way you did when you came here?
C
S: (No, I used to study with my friends. (Now I study alone.)
Do you live in the same place as when you first came?
Do you have a car? Is it the same kind that you had before?

Exercise continues on next page.

Do you have a checking/savings account? What did you have at home? Are they in the same bank as when you first came?
Do you have a lot of friends? As many as when you first came?
How did you get help when you first came? Is it the same now?
Do you read the U.S. newspapers? Did you when you first came?

SUMMARY DIALOGUE

Credit Cards

Chen and Nancy are discussing credit cards.

1. Chen: Nancy, can you help me with this?

2. Nancy: What is it?

3. Chen: A credit card.

4. Nancy: What's the matter with it?

5. Chen: Nothing, I guess. I got it from one of the large department stores. I took the card to the manager, but I didn't understand him. He spoke too fast. So now I have a card, but how do I use it?

6. Nancy: Can I have a look at it?

7. Chen: Sure, here, do I have to pay for it?

8. Nancy: Department stores don't usually have a fee.

9. Chen: Then, what if I find something in the store and I take it to the clerk?

10. Nancy: The clerk will probably say, "Is this cash or charge?" You'll say "charge," and she'll write out the charge slip. You'll sign it and keep a copy. Once a month the store will send you a bill.

11. Chen: Do they charge interest?

12. Nancy: Not if you pay on time. But if you're late, they'll charge you 1½% per month.

13. Chen: Per month! That's 18% a year! I don't want to pay that much.

14. Nancy: But the card is so convenient. You might see something really great, and you might not have any money.

15. Chen: Like what?

16. Nancy: I don't know, Chen! It's up to you. Kaufmann's is having a sale this weekend. Did you know that?

17. Chen: What's on sale?

18. Nancy: All kinds of stuff. Videogames for one thing.

19. Chen: Yeah? Well, maybe I ought to try my new credit card.

20. Nancy: Right, but remember you have to pay the bill some time.

COMMUNICATIVE ACTIVITIES

1) Discussion. Are credit cards commonly used in your country? Which ones are most popular? Do department stores have credit cards? Have you (or anyone you know) ever lost a credit card? What happened? What kinds of things do people use their credit cards for? Some people in the U.S. think it is morally wrong to use credit when you don't have money. What is the attitude in your country about people who do?

2) Problems.

Note to teachers: Divide students into appropriate sized groups and have a and b done as roleplays; c should be in the form of a report.

a) You're in a department store and find something you want. Take it to the clerk and charge it.

b) A very good friend always buys things using his credit card whether or not s/he has enough money. Persuade your friend that this is not a good idea.

c) Someone stole your wallet and credit cards. Find out what to do and how to do it. Find out what will happen if the thief charges items on your card.

Appendix

Phonetic Symbols

CONSONANTS

Symbol	*Example*	*Symbol*	*Example*
[p]	pit	[b]	bit
[t]	tin	[d]	din
[k]	cat	[g]	gun
[č]	church	[ǰ]	judge
[f]	fun	[v]	van
[θ]	thin	[ð]	then
[s]	sun	[z]	zoo
[š]	shirt	[ž]	azure
[m]	man	[n]	no
[ŋ]	sing	[r̥]	run
[l]	leg	[w]	win
[y]	yes	[h]	his

VOWELS

Symbol	*Example*
[i]	eat
[ɪ]	it
[e]	ate
[ɛ]	let
[æ]	at
[ə]	but
[ɒ]	lot
[u]	loot
[ʊ]	hook
[ɔ]	bought
[aɪ]	right
[aʊ]	out
[ɔɪ]	boy

INDEX OF PATTERNS

The grammatical patterns have been indexed alphabetically according to the traditional terminology found in most handbooks of English grammar. The first number following each entry refers to the lesson in which the item first appears as a teaching point; the second number refers to the page. The index includes the patterns from both Part 1 (Lessons 1–11) and Part 2 (Lessons 12–22).